DEAR GOD KIDS ™

™ Designates a Trademark of INTERCONTINENTAL GREETINGS, LTD.

© Copyright INTERCONTINENTAL GREETINGS, LTD., All Rights Reserved

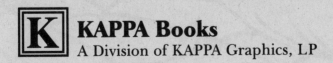

KAPPA Books
A Division of KAPPA Graphics, LP

Copyright ©2004 by Kappa Books, a division of Kappa Graphics, LP.
No part of this book may be reproduced or copied without written permission of the publisher.
All rights reserved. Printed in the UNITED STATES OF AMERICA.

Dear God,
GOOD MORNING

Dear God,

THANKS FOR MAKING ME

Annie ©

Dear God,
...You should have asked me first if I wanted freckles

Dear God,
You should have asked me if I wanted
freckles.

Freckles, long eyelashes, dimpled cheeks,
curly hair - these are the things that set
you apart, that make you like no one else
in the whole wide world. Even if you could
trade them in on something else, maybe in
a different color or shape, you wouldn't look
like yourself anymore. And being yourself
is the greatest way to say "Thanks, God, for
making me."

I will praise thee, for I am
fearfully and wonderfully made.
Psalm 139:14

Dear God,

WHAT A GREAT IDEA TO MAKE US ALL DIFFERENT!

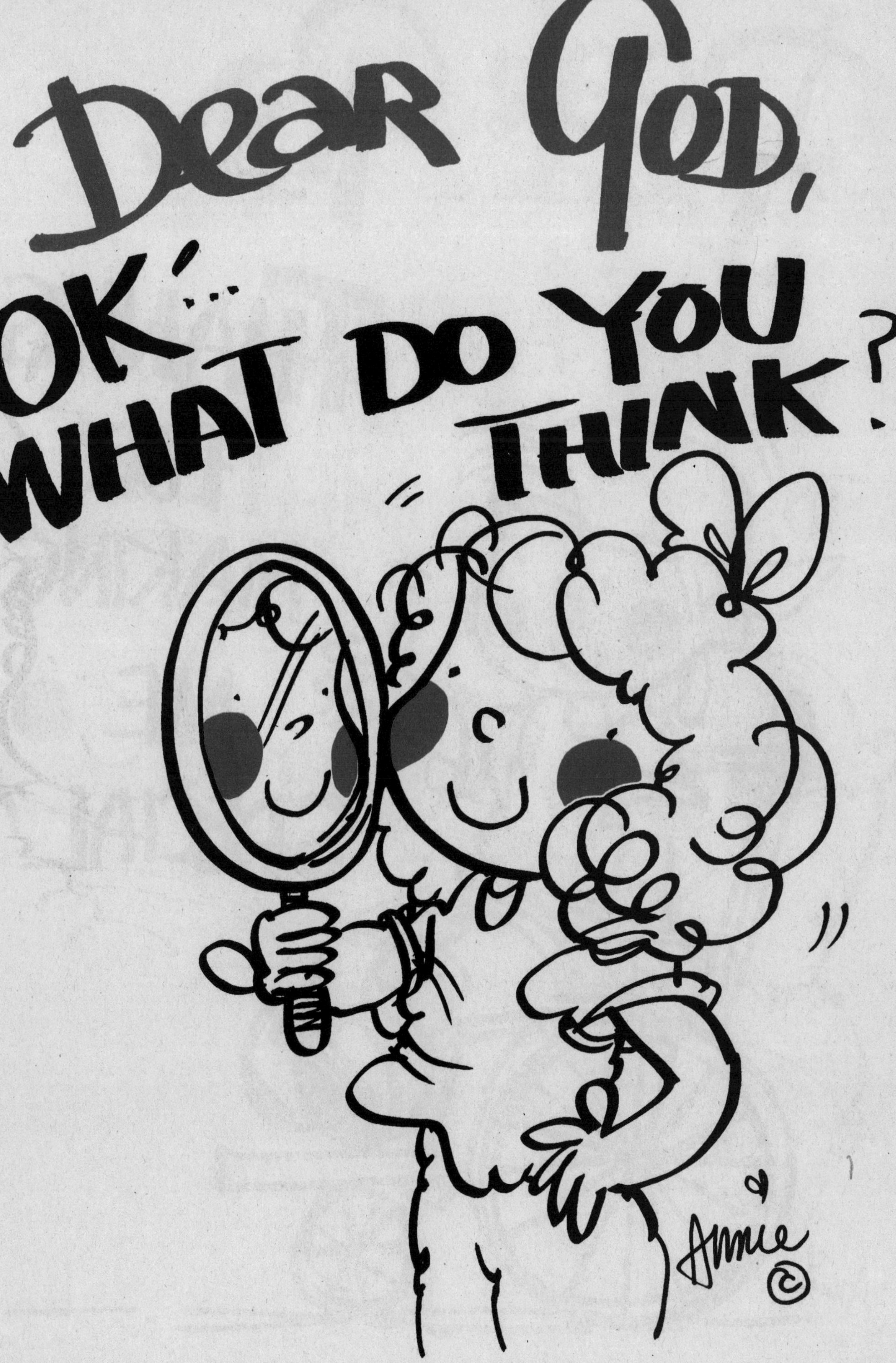
DEAR GOD,
OK'... WHAT DO YOU THINK?
Annie ©

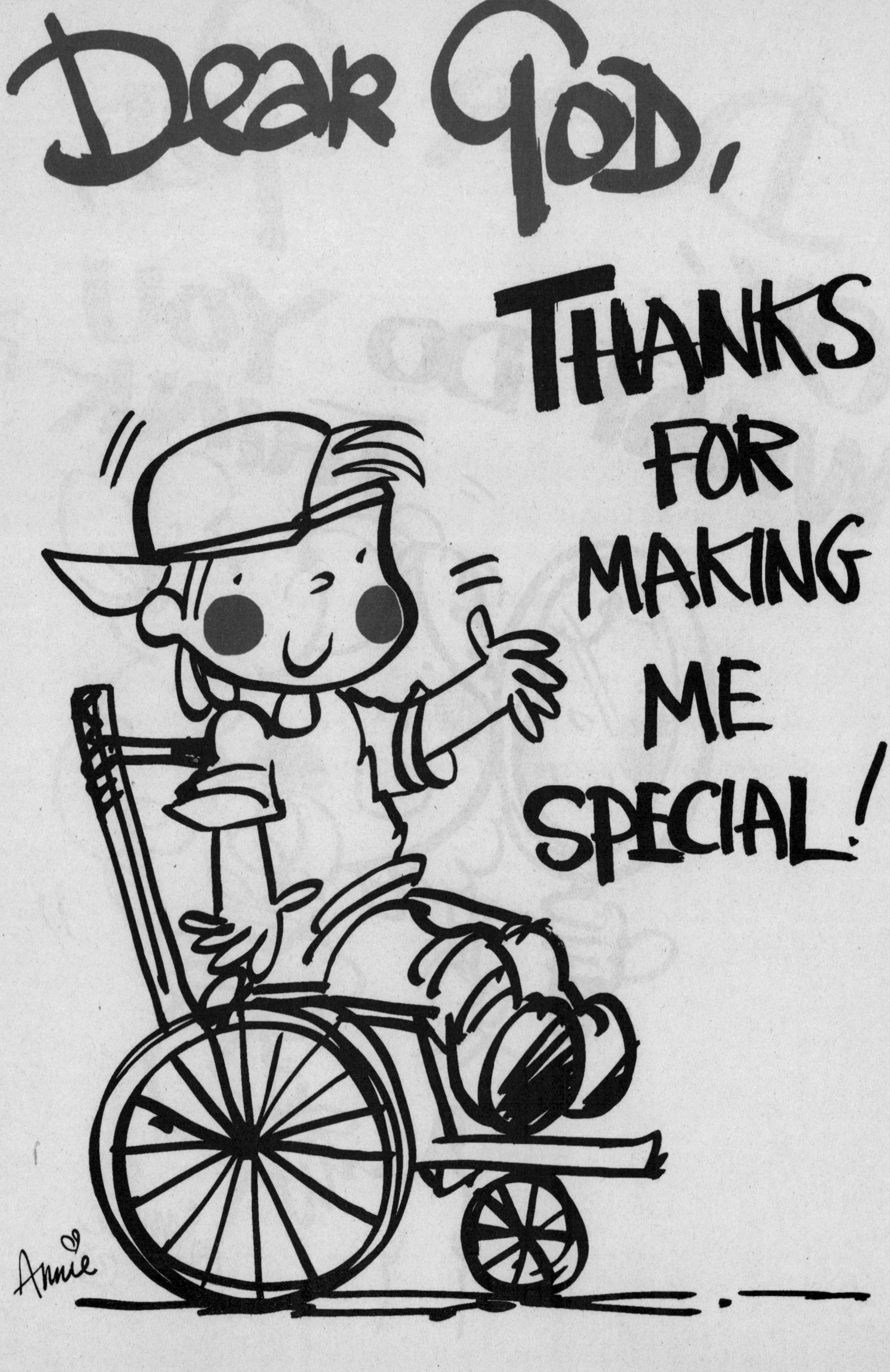
DEAR GOD,
THANKS FOR MAKING ME SPECIAL!
Annie

Dear God,
Thanks for making me special!

Everybody has things they can't do very
well, like climbing a rope at the playground,
doing tricks with a yo-yo, or drawing decent-
looking hands in a picture. But it's a lot
easier to be mad about the things you can't
do than to thank God for the things you can.
With a little work, you can get better at
some of that stuff. With a thankful heart,
you can be your best at everything.

For I have learned, in whatsoever
state I am, therewith to be content.
Philippians 4:11

Dear God,

WE MAY BE TWINS ... BUT WE'VE GOT OUR VERY OWN MINDS

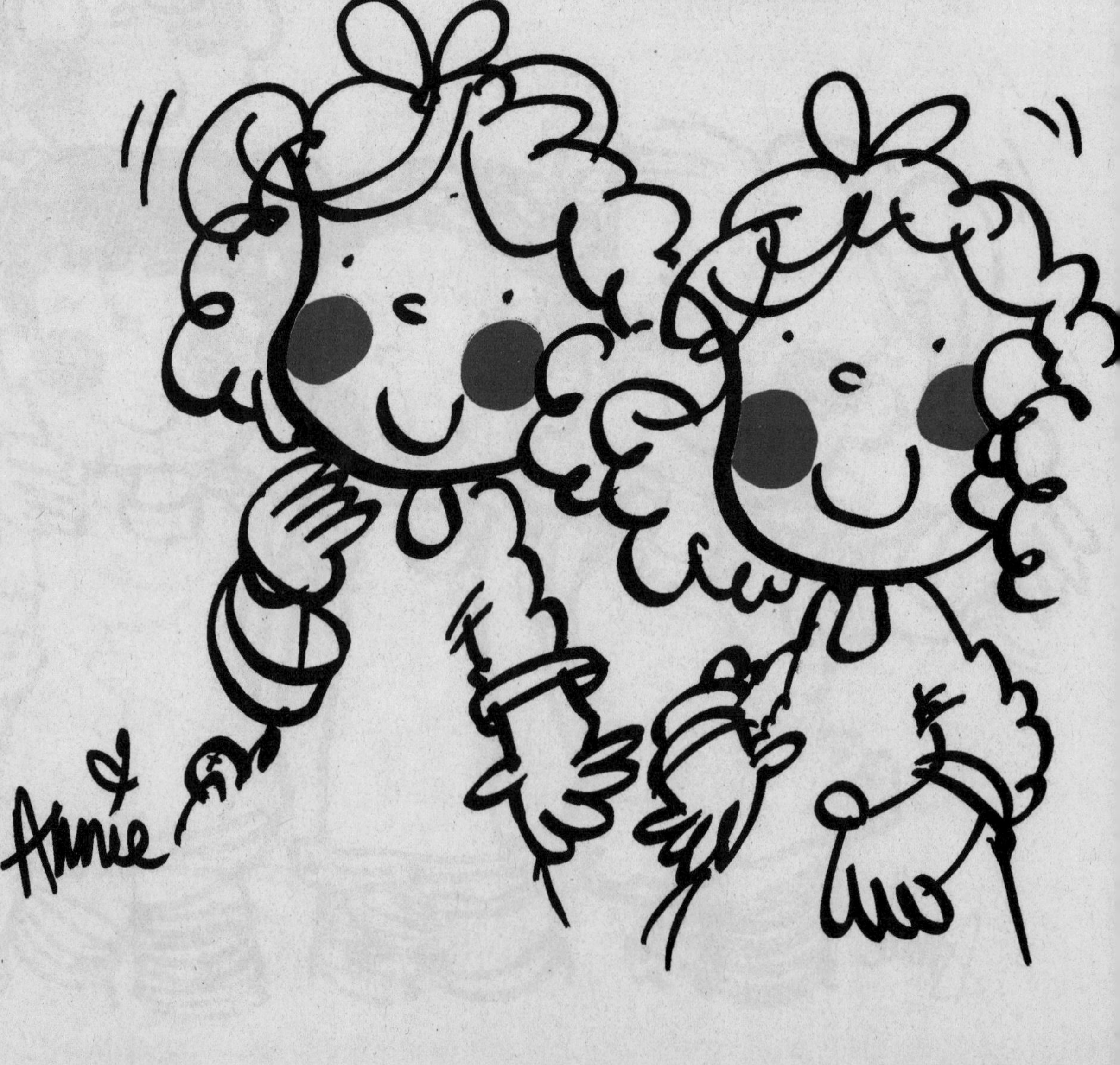

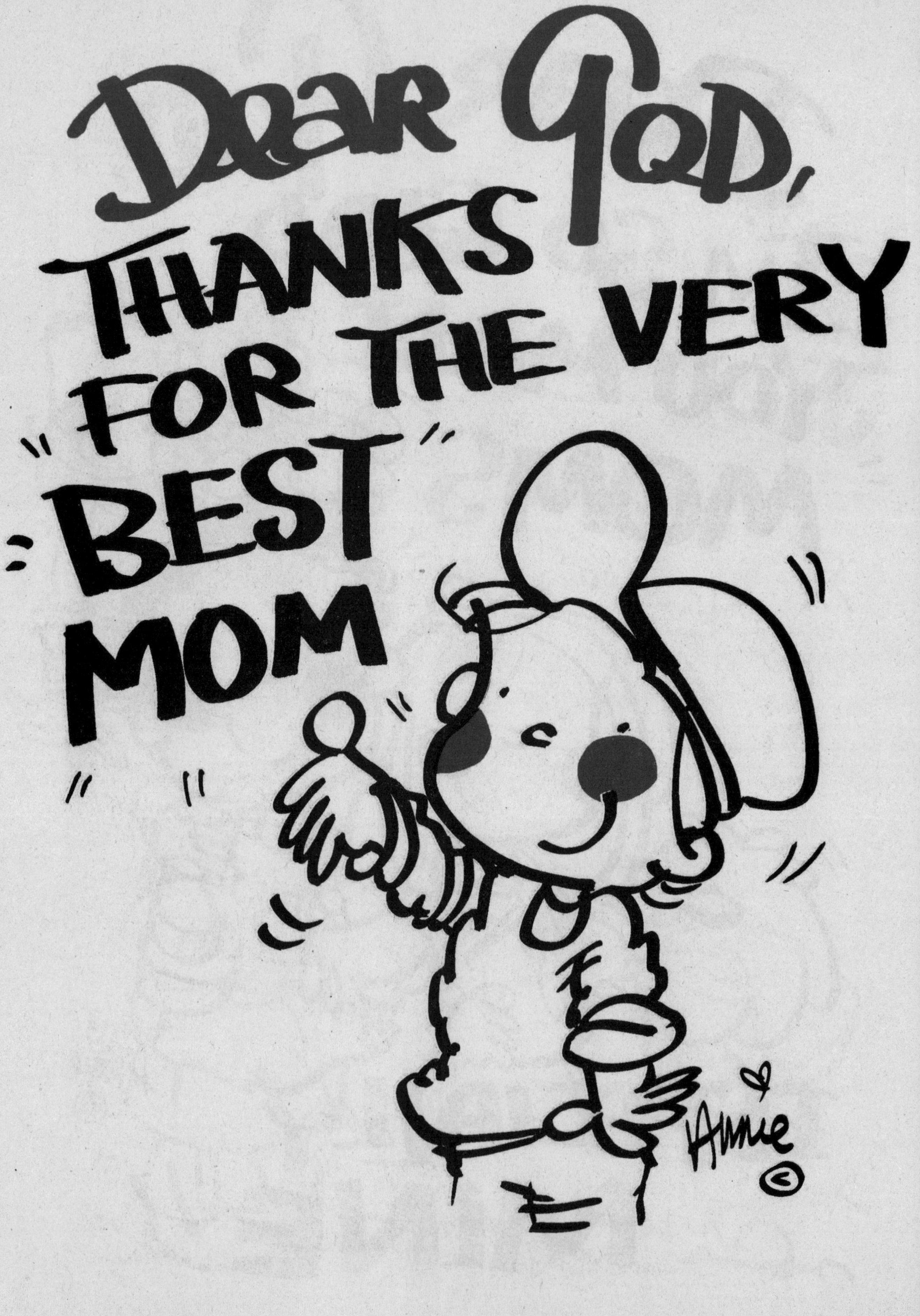
DEAR GOD,
THANKS FOR THE VERY
"BEST"
MOM
Annie ©

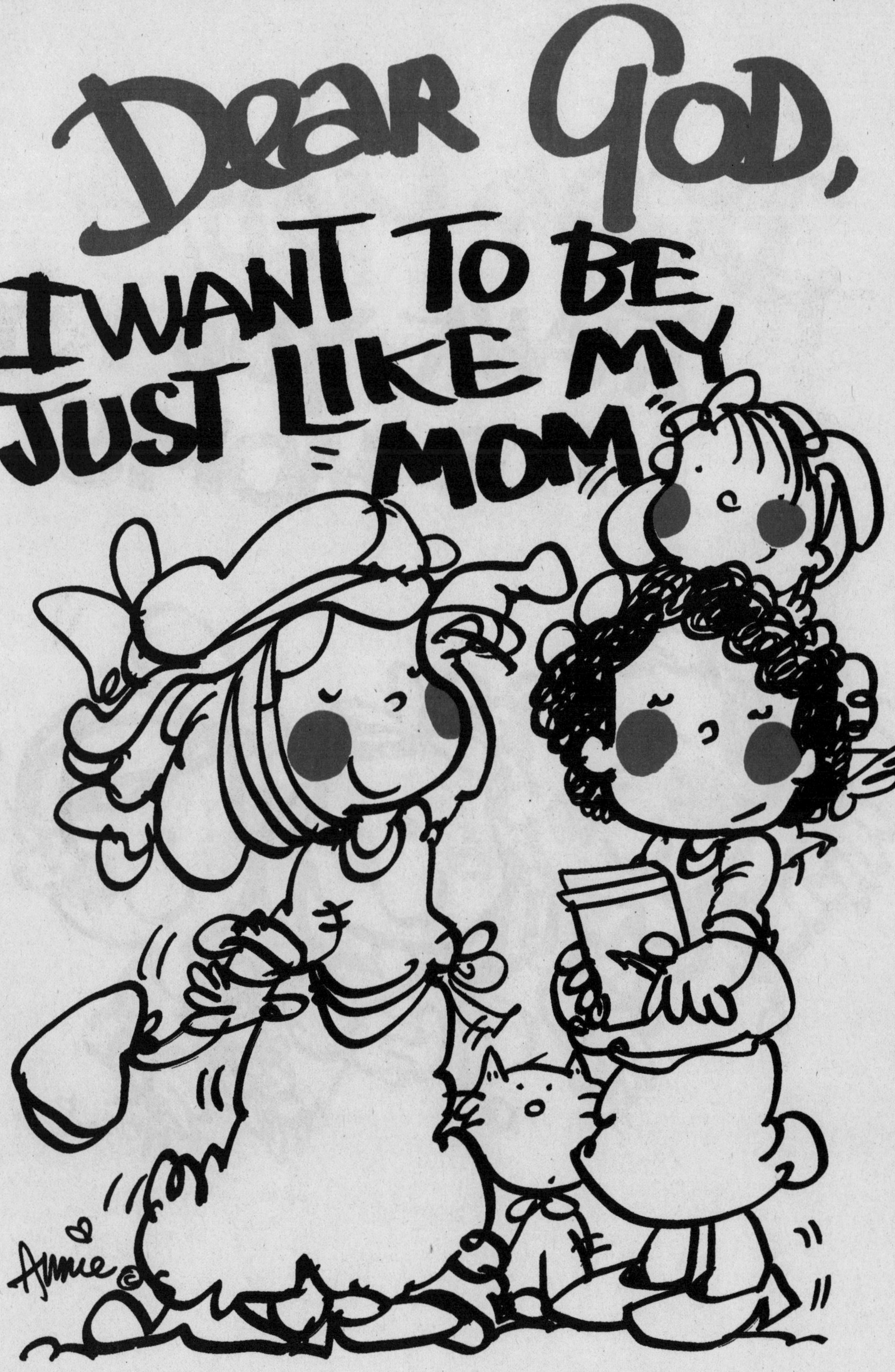
Dear God,
I WANT TO BE
JUST LIKE MY
MOM
Annie ©

Dear God, Thank You For Moms

Dear God,
Thank you for Moms!

What would your mornings be like without your mom? Who would be there to wake you up, make you breakfast, and smother you with kisses? The world functions better because of the love and compassion of mommies. God has blessed us with mothers and fathers. He tells us to obey and respect our parents. The next time Mom tells you to pick up your toys, or fold the towels, or eat your vegetables, make sure you obey. Your mother knows what's best for you. Think of it this way, by obeying your mom, you are obeying God!

Honor thy father and thy mother: that thy days may be long upon the land which the Lord thy God giveth thee.

Exodus 20:12

Dear God, I've got the best mom in the whole world... thanks!!

Annie

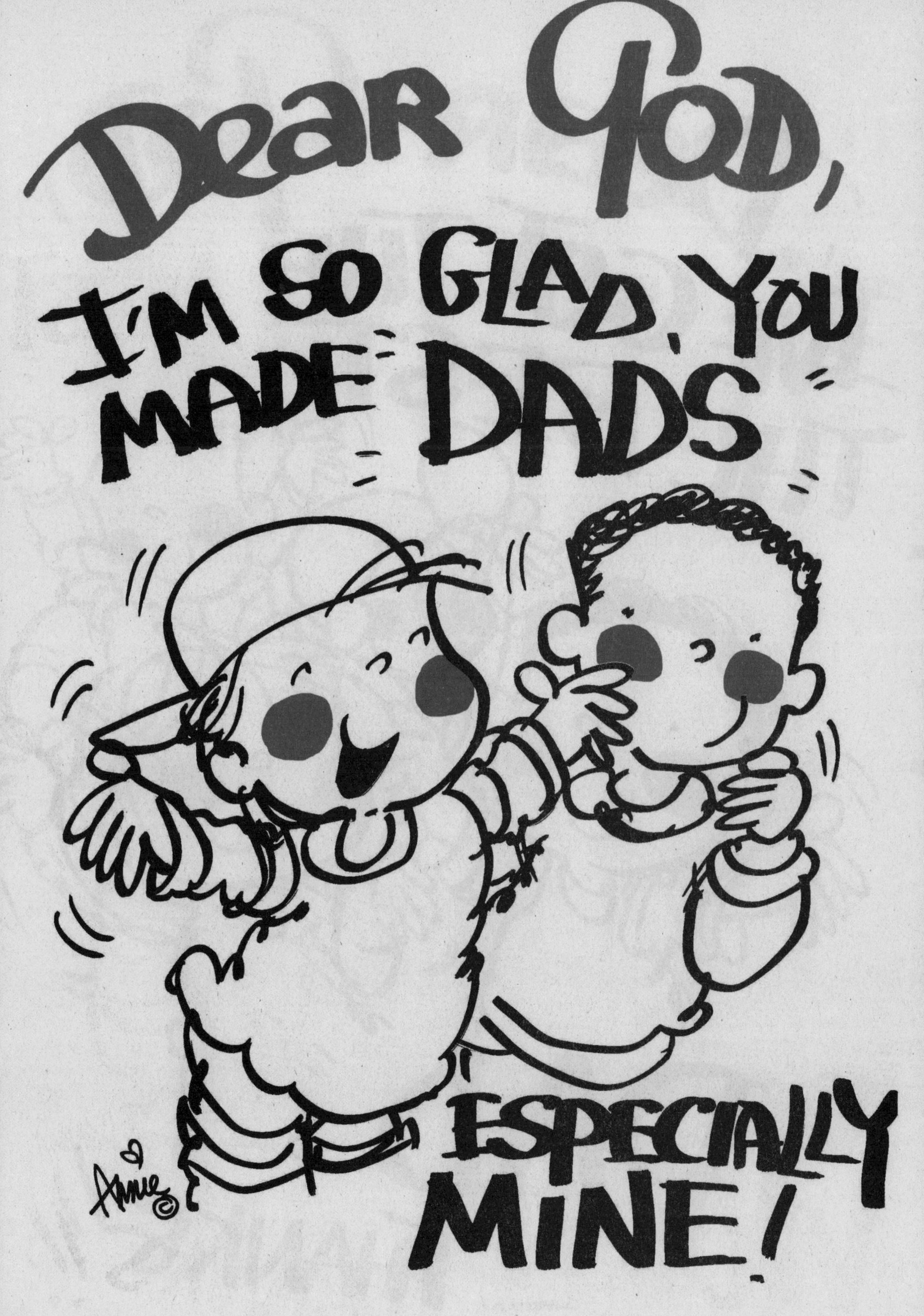
DEAR GOD,
I'M SO GLAD YOU MADE DADS
ESPECIALLY MINE!
Annie ©

Dear God,
I've got the best Dad. Thanks!"

God put your dad in your life to love, teach
and support you. Dads work hard so you and
your family can have food, clothing, and
shelter. Daddy shows his love by the way he
cares for you. Did you know that you have
"two daddies"? Yes, God is your Heavenly
daddy. He loves you, too! He protects you
from evil and watches out for you. You are
blessed to have an earthly daddy and a
heavenly daddy! Be sure to tell your daddy
that you love him! While you are at it, let
your Heavenly Father know that you love
Him, too!

*But now, O Lord, thou art our father; we are the clay,
and thou our potter; and we all are the work of thy hand.*

Isaiah 64:8

DEAR GOD,
THANKS! MY PARENTS ARE SO PROUD!
Annie ©

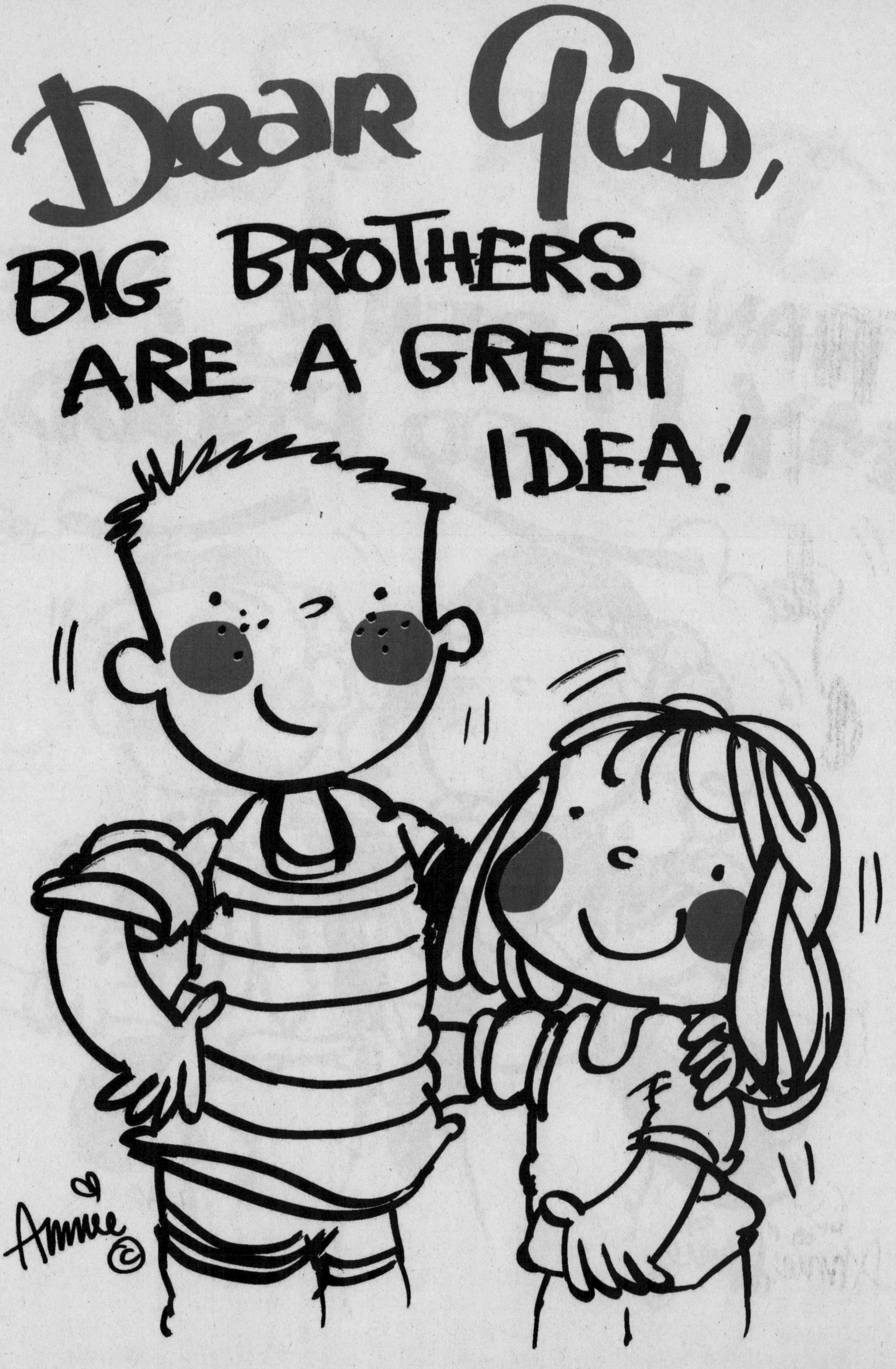
Dear God,
BIG BROTHERS ARE A GREAT IDEA!
Annie ©

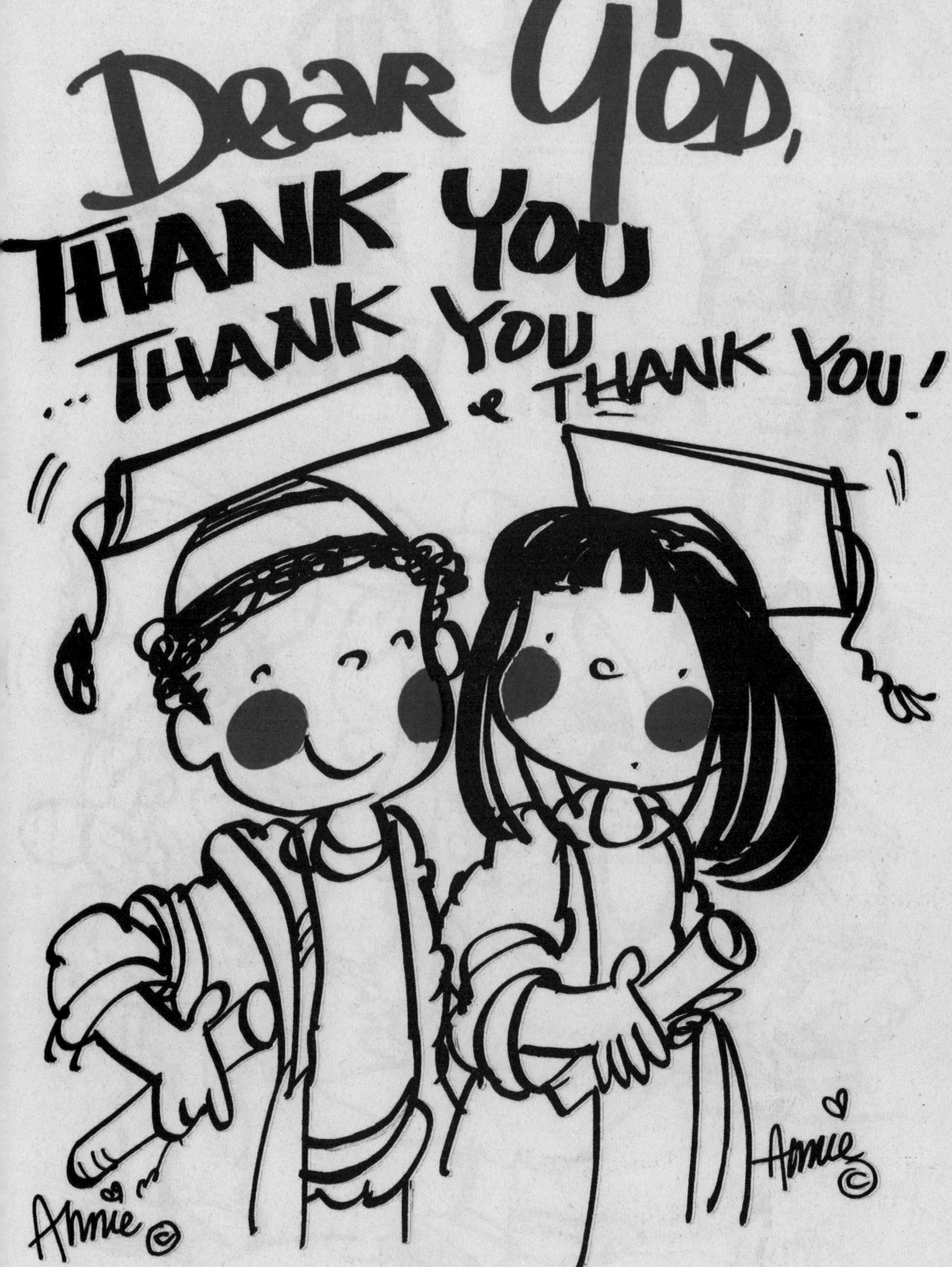

Dear God,

THEY MAY NOT BE THE REAL THING ... BUT I AM

Annie

Dear God,
They may not be the real thing, but I am.

When you're pretending, you can be anything.
You can win a gold medal in the 100 - yard
dash or make the winning score in a basket-
ball game. But God sees you the way you
really are, and He thinks you're incredible
even when you're not defending an island fort
that's been surrounded by pirates. The
person you are is the person he loves.

How precious also are thy thoughts unto me, O God!
How great is the sum of them!
Psalm 139:17

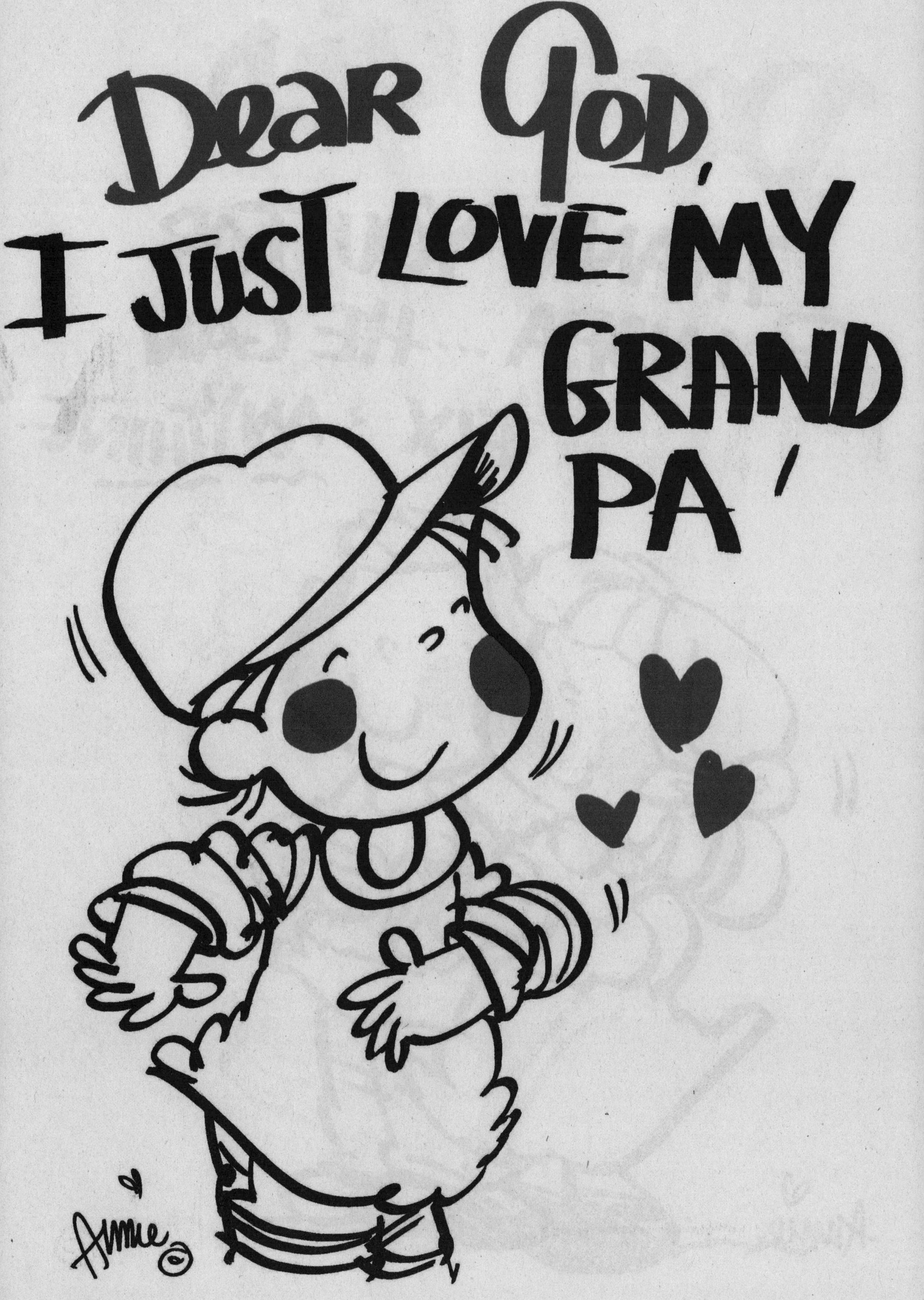
DEAR GOD,
I JUST LOVE MY GRAND PA!
Annie ©

DEAR GOD,

THANK YOU FOR GRANDPA ... HE CAN FIX "ANYTHING"

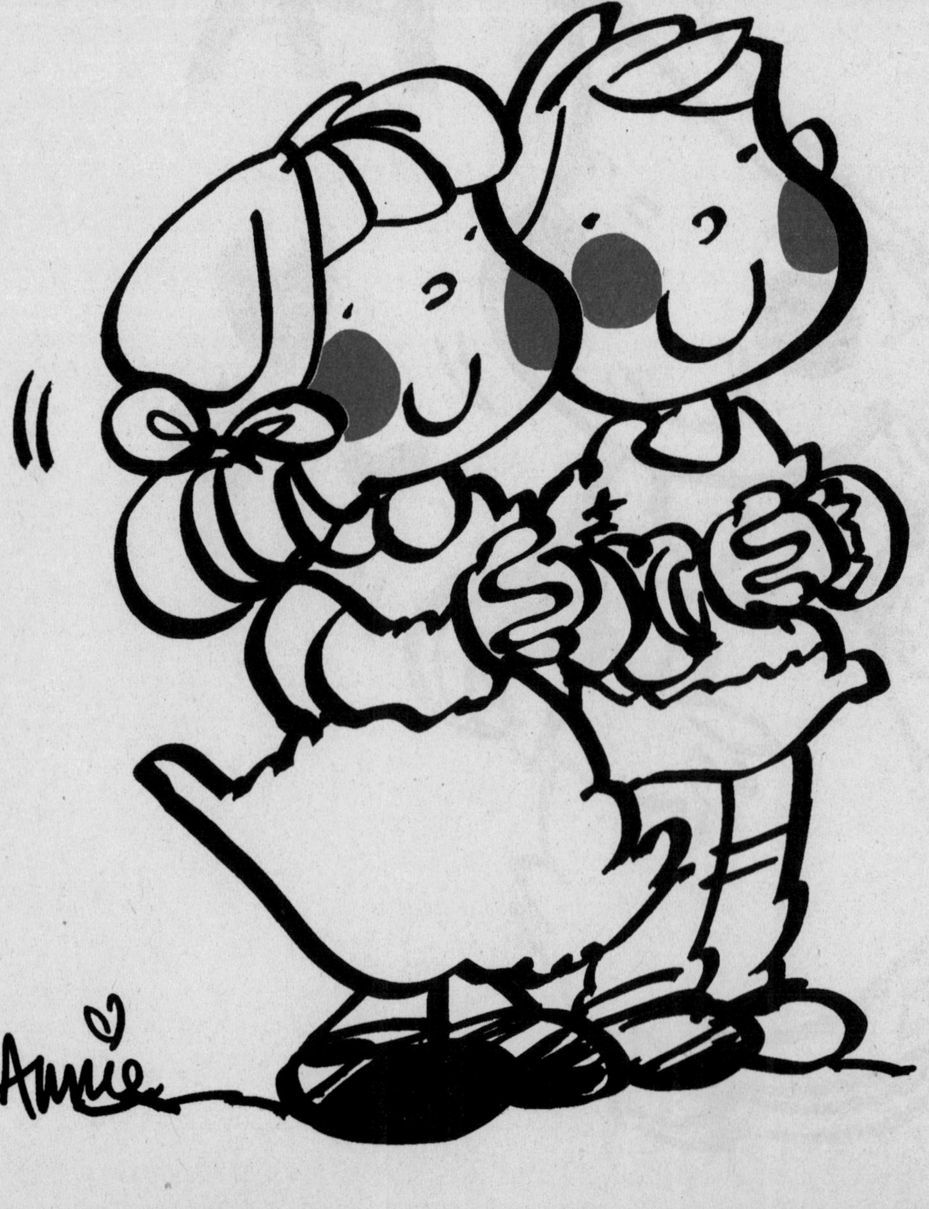

Dear God,
Thank you for Grandpa . . . he can fix
anything!

When you think of your grandpa, do you see
fishing poles, a football, or a funny hat? Your
grandpa is a wise man. He has lived a long
time, and has learned a lot.

God wants us to be wise, too. God told King
Solomon that He would bless him with what-
ever he wanted. Solomon could have asked for
money, or a big house. Instead, he asked for
wisdom. God was pleased with this answer.
In return, He blessed him with wisdom and
many good things.

The glory of young men is their strength, and the
honor of old men is their gray hair.

Proverbs 20:29 (NASB)

Dear God,

'Tis not easy to stay quiet about some things

Dear God, THANK YOU FOR TEACHERS

Annie

Dear God,
Thank you for Teachers!

It is a privilege to learn important subjects like history, writing, and math. Teachers work hard to help you understand this information. Teachers instruct you in school topics, but the greatest subject you can ever learn is the Word of God. The Bible will help you have a closer relationship with God. And God has promised that He will help you learn. By praying and studying God's Word, you can be a student of the best teacher of all, God!

I will instruct you and teach you in the way you should go; I will counsel you and watch over you.

Psalm 32:8 (NIV)

DEAR GOD,
WHEN YOU CARE
...IT
SHOWS

Annie ©

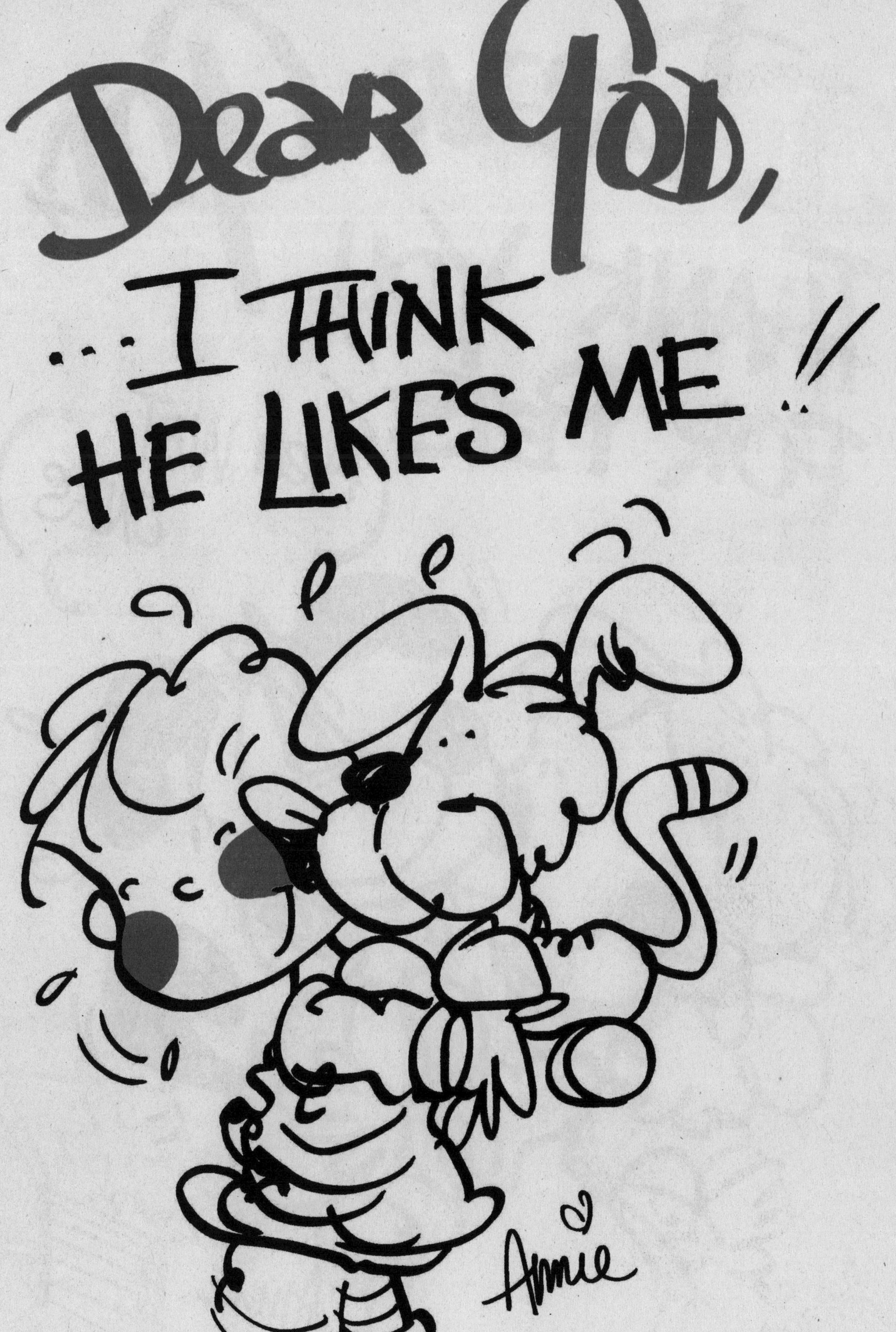
Dear God,
...I THINK HE LIKES ME!!
Annie

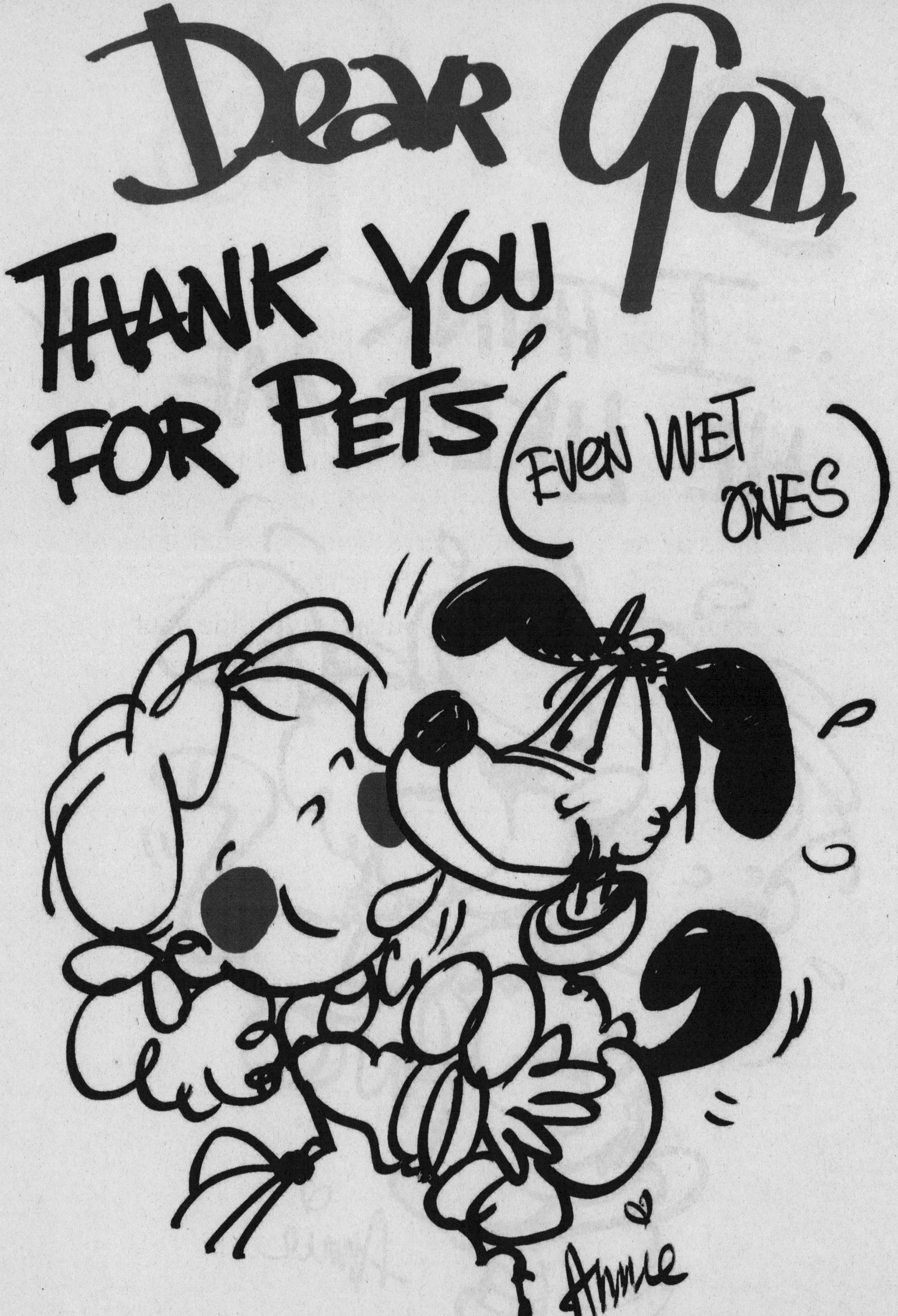
DEAR GOD
THANK YOU FOR PETS
(EVEN WET ONES)
Annie

Dear God,
Thank you for pets (even wet ones).

Cats and dogs are great friends and companions. They make you laugh and keep you entertained. You take good care of your pets because you love them. Just as you are the master of your pet, God is the master of all of us. He created you and will guide your life. Your pet trusts you to feed and shelter it. You can put your trust in God. He will always take care of you!

He shall feed his flock like a shepherd; he shall gather the lambs with his arm, and carry them in his bosom, and shall gently lead those that are with young.

Isaiah 40:11

DEAR GOD,
I THINK I FOUND A FRIEND

Annie ©

Dear God,

Friends Are Special!

Dear God,
I THINK IV'E FOUND A FRIEND

Annie ©

Dear God,

I'VE GOT A BEST FRIEND

Dear God, Thank you "for friends".

Annie

Dear God,
Thank you for friends.

You've come to the right place by thanking
God for your friends, because He's the one
who's given them to you. Back when you
didn't know each other, before you'd even
seen each other, God worked it out so that
you and your friends could get together.
Whenever you think about how glad you are
to have the friends you do, give God a great
big "thank you."

Stand every morning to thank and
praise the Lord, and likewise at evening.
1 Chronicles 23:30

Dear God,
I THINK MY FRIEND IS THE "BEST"

DEAR GOD,

IT'S GREAT TO HAVE A FRIEND

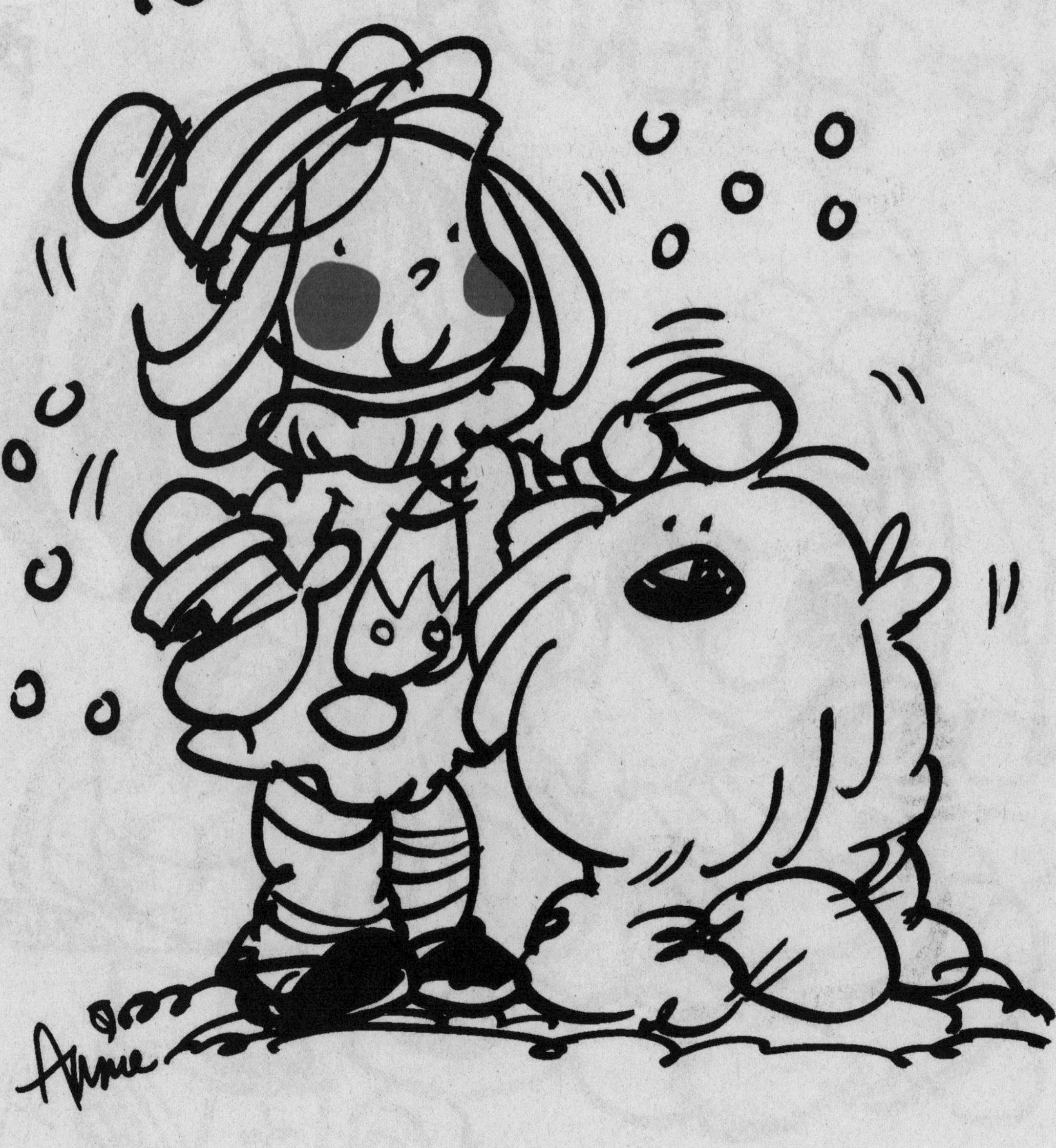

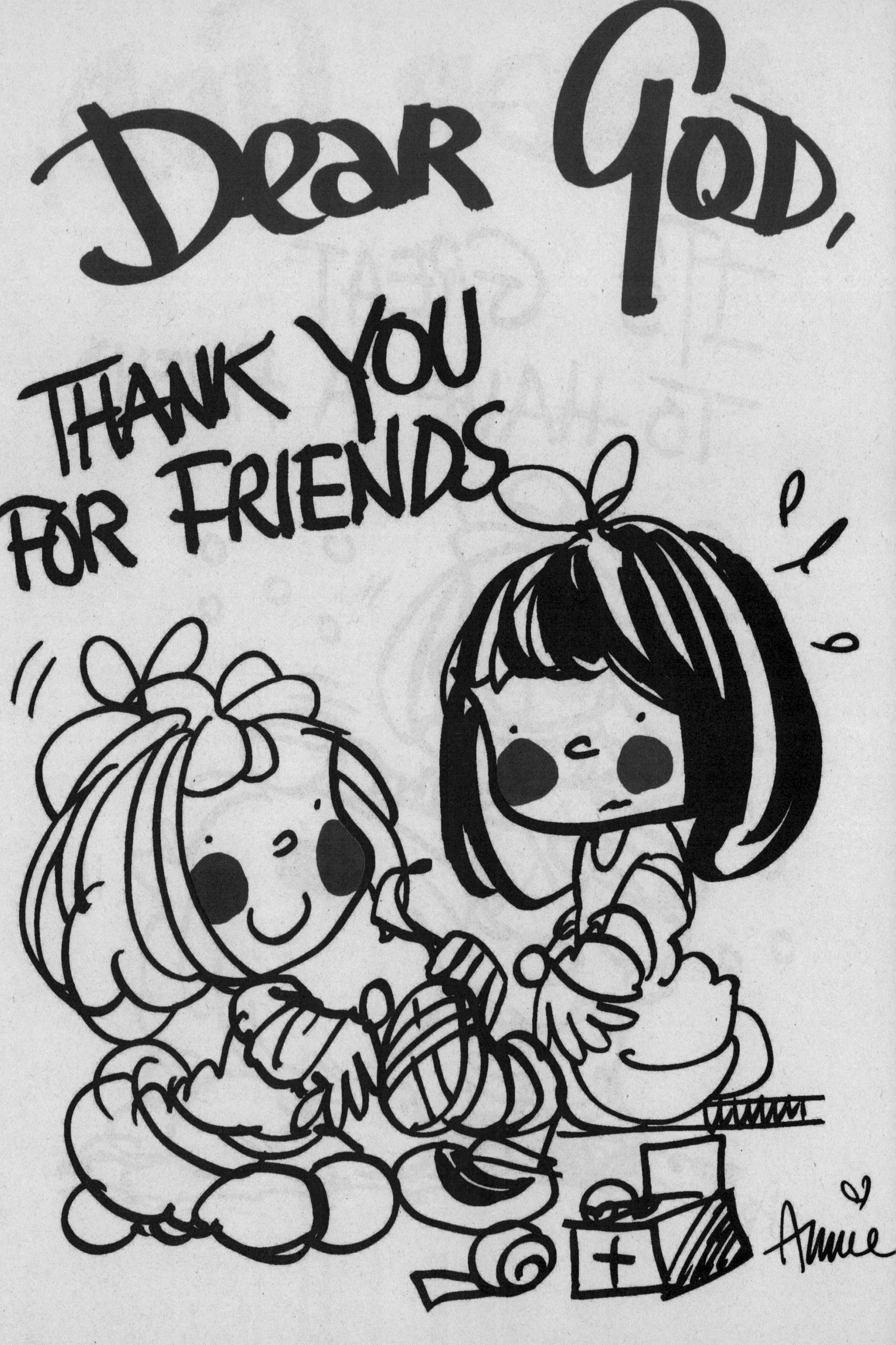

Dear God,
THANK YOU FOR FRIENDS
Annie

Dear God,
Thank you for friends.

You can go to a friend when you're having a
good day or a bad day. Friends are wonderful
gifts that God has put in your life for
support and fun. Friends will pass in and
out of your life. But there is one friend who
will stick with you forever, God! God wants
to be your best friend. You can confide in
Him and tell Him secrets! Everything in your
life will be much better when you ask God
to be your best friend.

A man that hath friends must show himself friendly,
and there is a friend that sticketh closer than a brother.

Proverbs 18:24

DEAR GOD, I HAVE SO MUCH TO TELL YOU!

Annie ©

Dear God, REAL FRIENDS ARE THERE WHEN YOU NEED THEM!

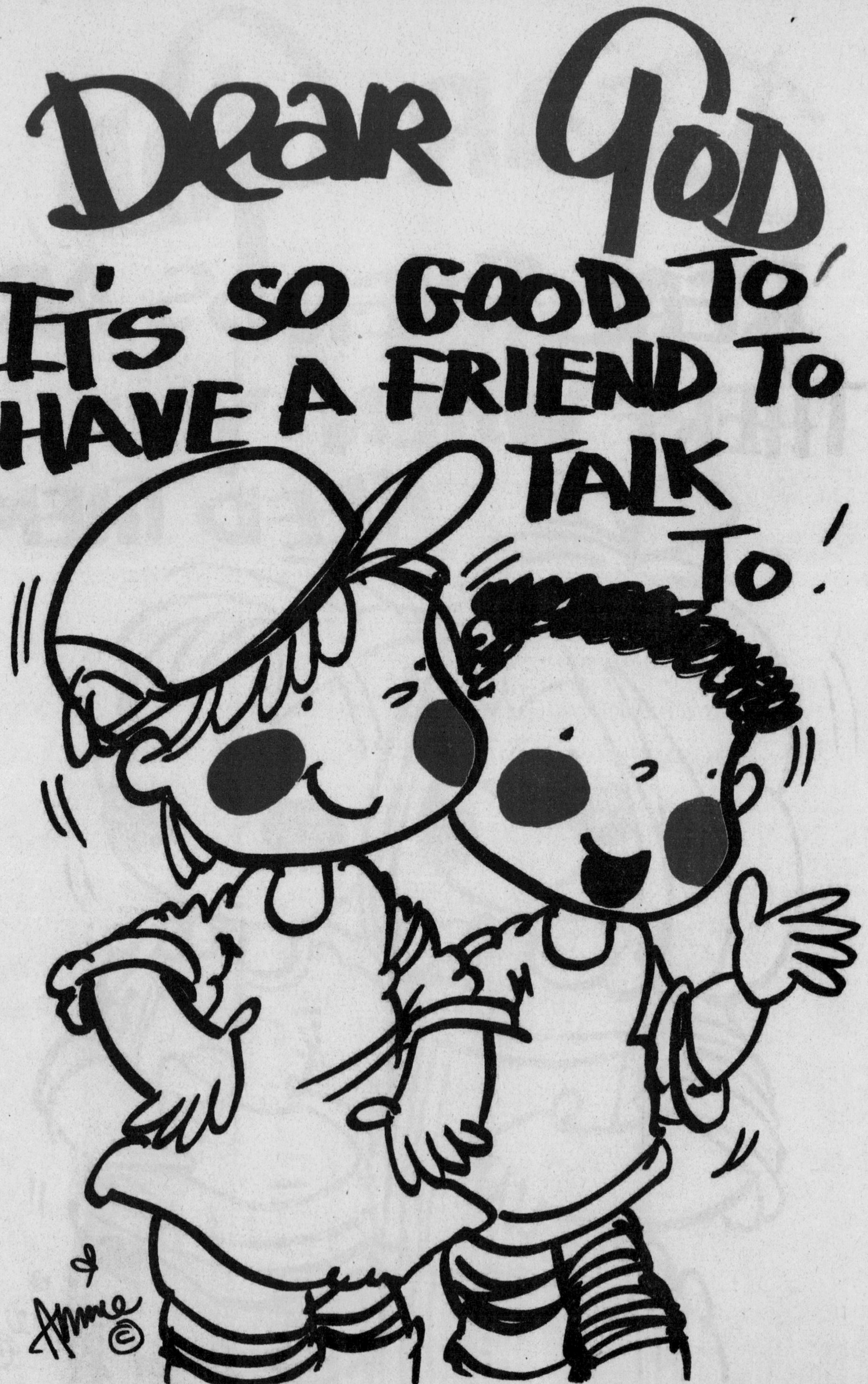
DEAR GOD
IT'S SO GOOD TO HAVE A FRIEND TO TALK TO!
Annie ©

Dear God,
A real friend is someone who takes time
to listen to you.

It's a whole lot easier to talk than to listen.
It's a whole lot more fun to tell what **you**
got for Christmas than to hear what **they**
got. It's a whole lot harder to care what
somebody **else** thinks when **you** think you
haven't been treated fair. But how great
it is to have a friend who'll listen when you
feel like talking - or to be a friend who
listens to what others need to say.

Trust in him at all times; ye people, pour out
your heart before him. God is a refuge for us.
Psalm 62:8

Dear God, We Need To Talk!

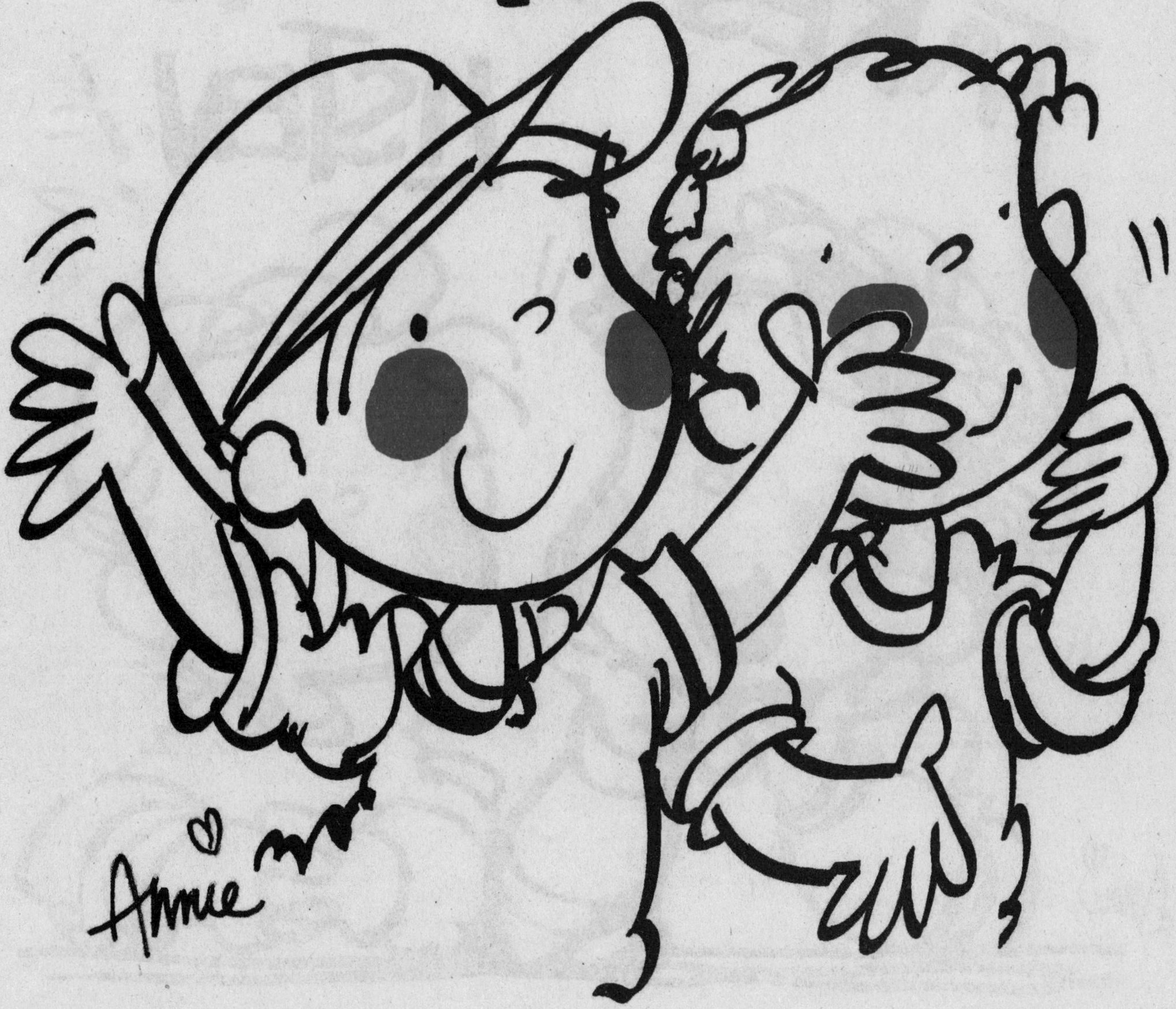

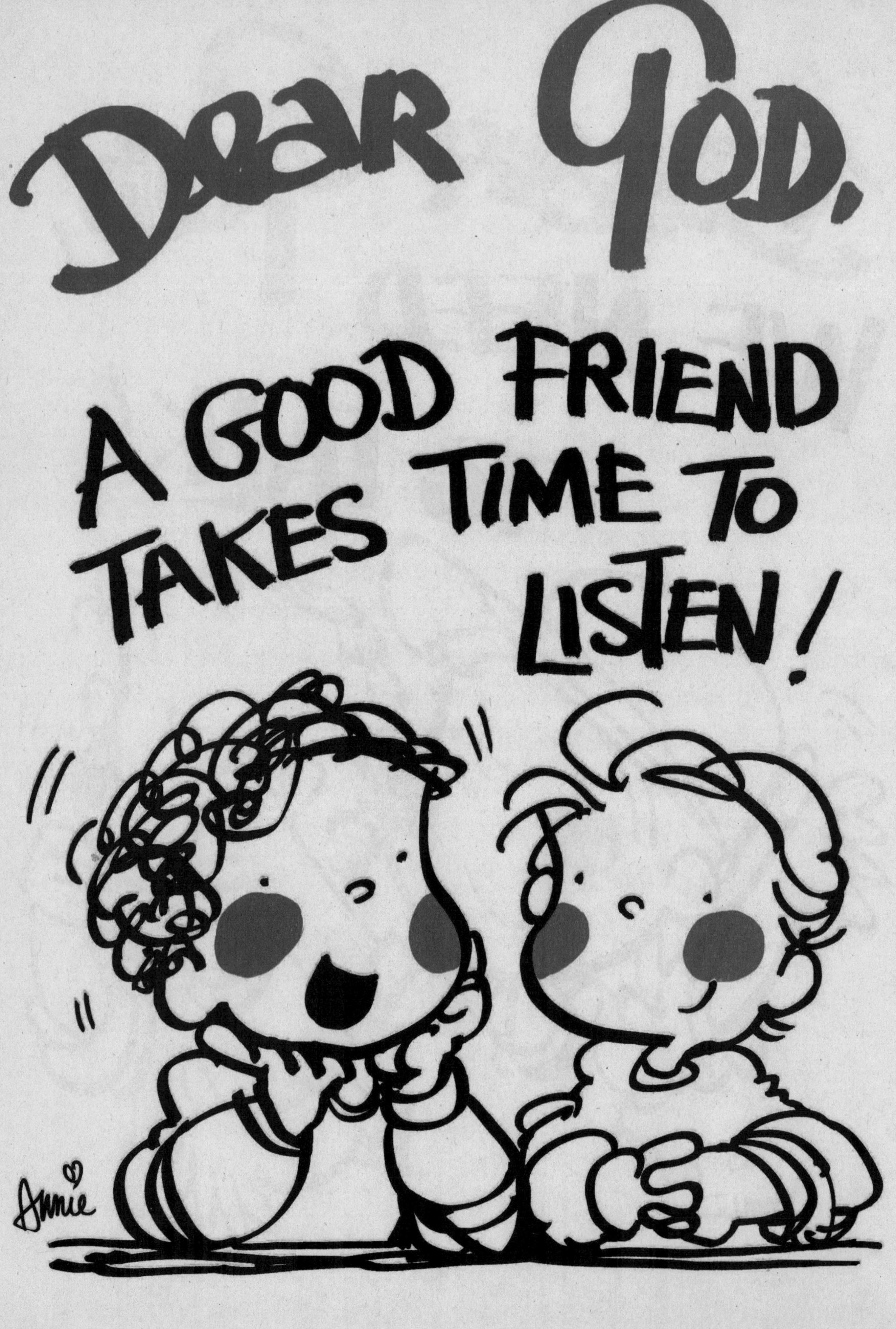
DEAR GOD,
A GOOD FRIEND TAKES TIME TO LISTEN!
Annie

Dear God,
A real friend is someone who takes time to listen to you.

The Lord is great! He is the best friend to have in life. He is never too busy to hear my prayer. He cares about the little details, as well as my big decisions. God loves me. I can trust His caring words of good advice. I can talk to Him about anything. I can talk to Him anywhere. I can talk to Him anytime. When I am alone, the Lord sees and hears me. He never leaves me.

"Hear me when I call, O God...have mercy upon me, and hear my prayer...the Lord will hear when I call unto him."
Psalm 4:1,3

Dear God,
Thank you for sharing with me, when I share with you.

I share my loaves and fishes with others. God gives me a Thanksgiving feast. If I give away all that I have, God gives me more than enough. The Lord is an awesome God. He is the best friend to share with others. I share my thoughts, feelings, and troubles with God. He gives me wisdom. He guides me with His Spirit. He teaches me through His Word. He shows me how to live a good life. I thank God for sharing with me, whenever I share with Him.

"Call unto me, and I will answer thee, and shew thee great and mighty things, which thou knowest not."
Jeremiah 33:3

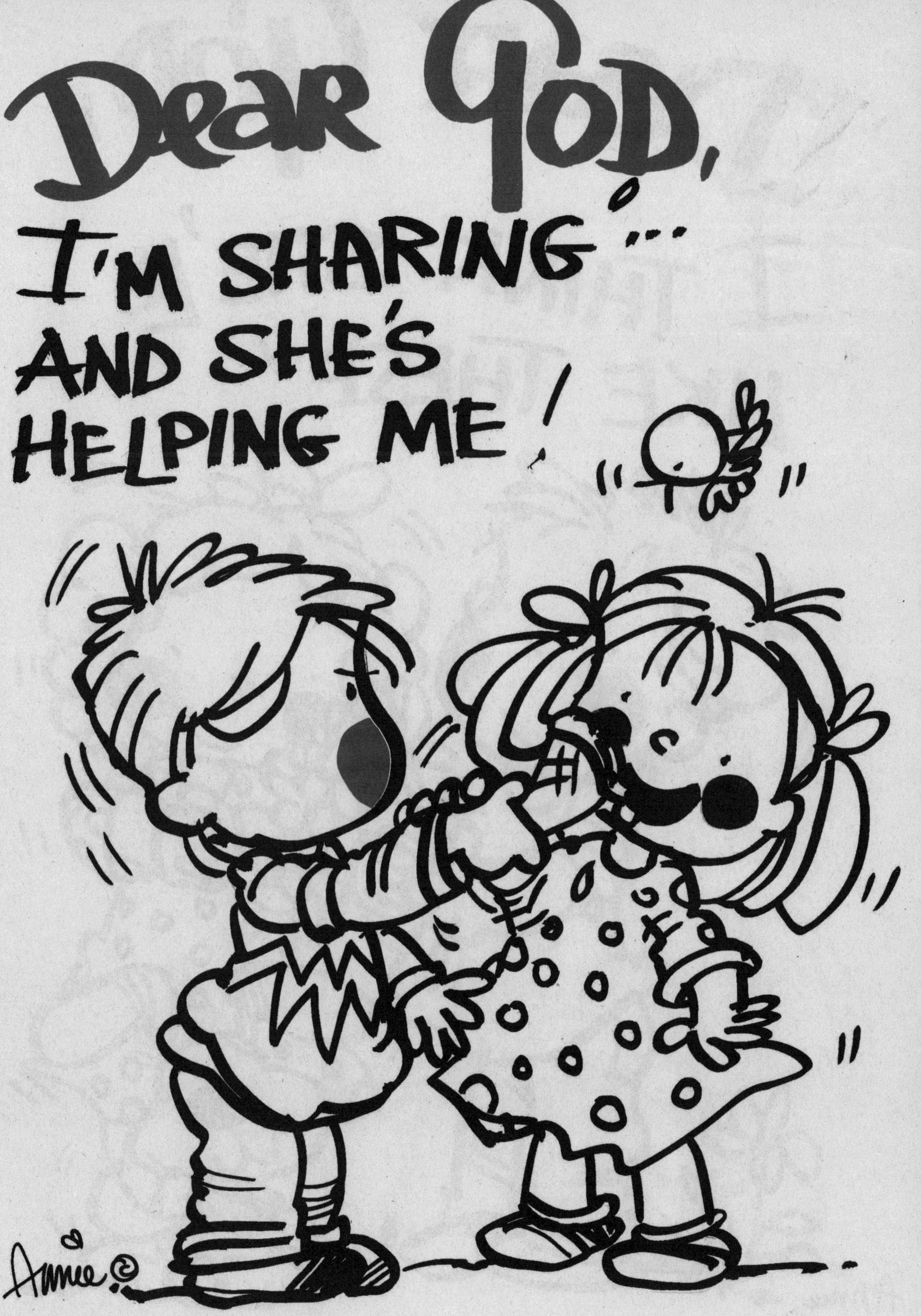
Dear God,
I'M SHARING...
AND SHE'S
HELPING ME!
Annie ©

DEAR GOD,
I THINK SHE'LL LIKE THESE!

Annie ©

DEAR GOD, THESE ARE FOR YOU!

Dear God,

I THINK I'VE GOT A GOOD FEELING

Annie

Dear God,
I think I've got a good feeling.

Friends are just fun all the way around.
School friends are great. So are the
friends who live near you. But some of your
best friends are the ones who live right in
your own home - your brother, your sister,
your family. And God, of course, is your
best friend of all, and He goes with you
everywhere you go - to keep you feeling
good just about anywhere you are.

The Lord hath done great things
for us, whereof we are glad.
Psalm 126:3

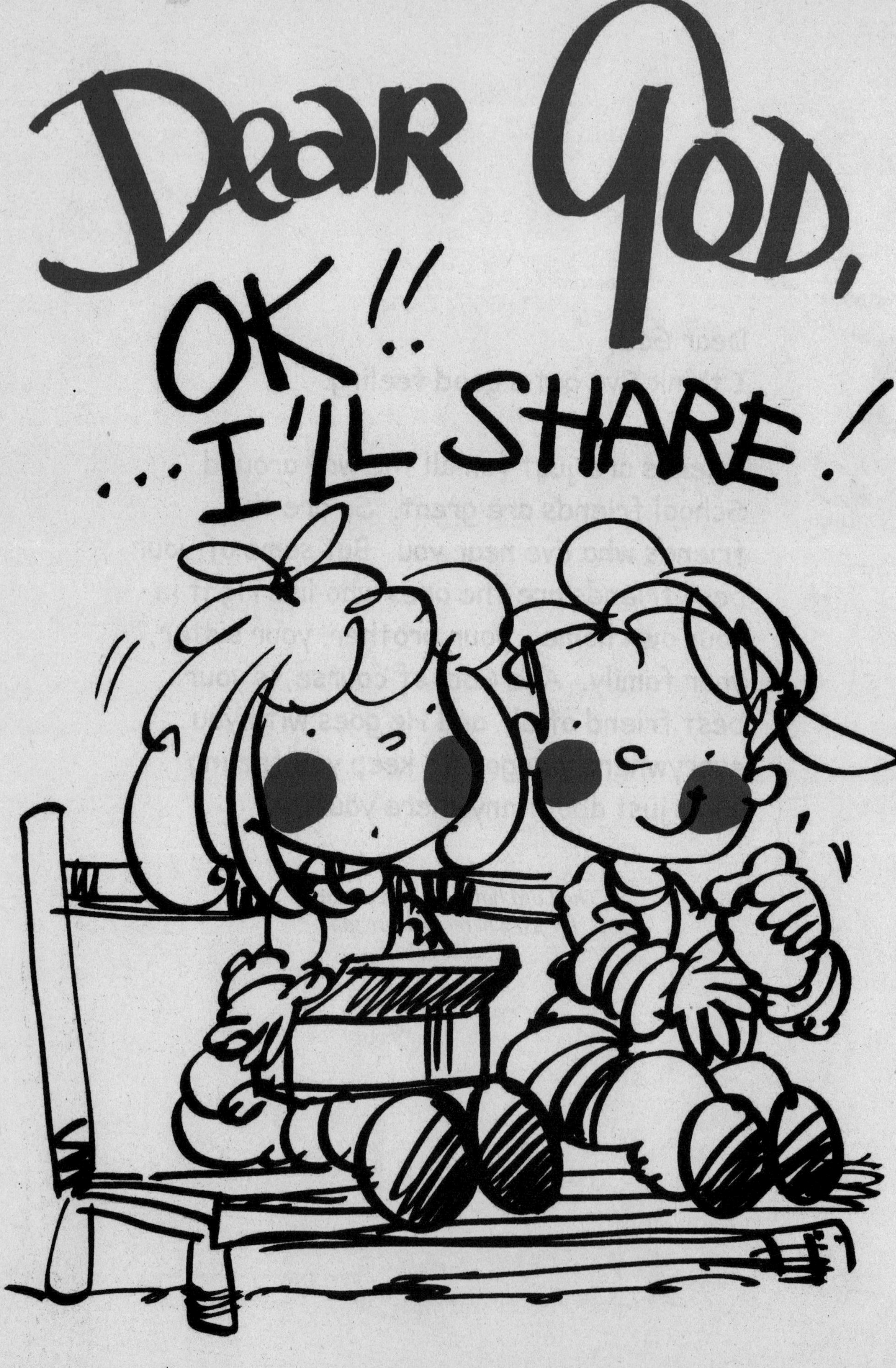
Dear God,
OK!! ... I'LL SHARE!

Dear God,
Thanks for Your help.

When I ask God for help, it is important that I remember to say, "Thank you." Praise and Thanksgiving please the heart of God. I tell God that I love Him for who He is by praising His name: I thank God for material blessings, such as warm clothes and a soft bed. I thank God for physical blessings, such as eyes to see the blue sky and ears to hear the birds sing. I thank God for spiritual blessings, such as love, forgiveness, wisdom and guidance. I thank God for the people in the world around me. I thank God for everything!

"...in every thing by prayer and supplication with thanksgiving let your requests be made know unto God. And the peace of God, which passeth all understanding, shall keep your hearts and minds"
Philippians 4:6,7

Dear God, HELP ME TO MAKE GOOD USE OF MY TIME!

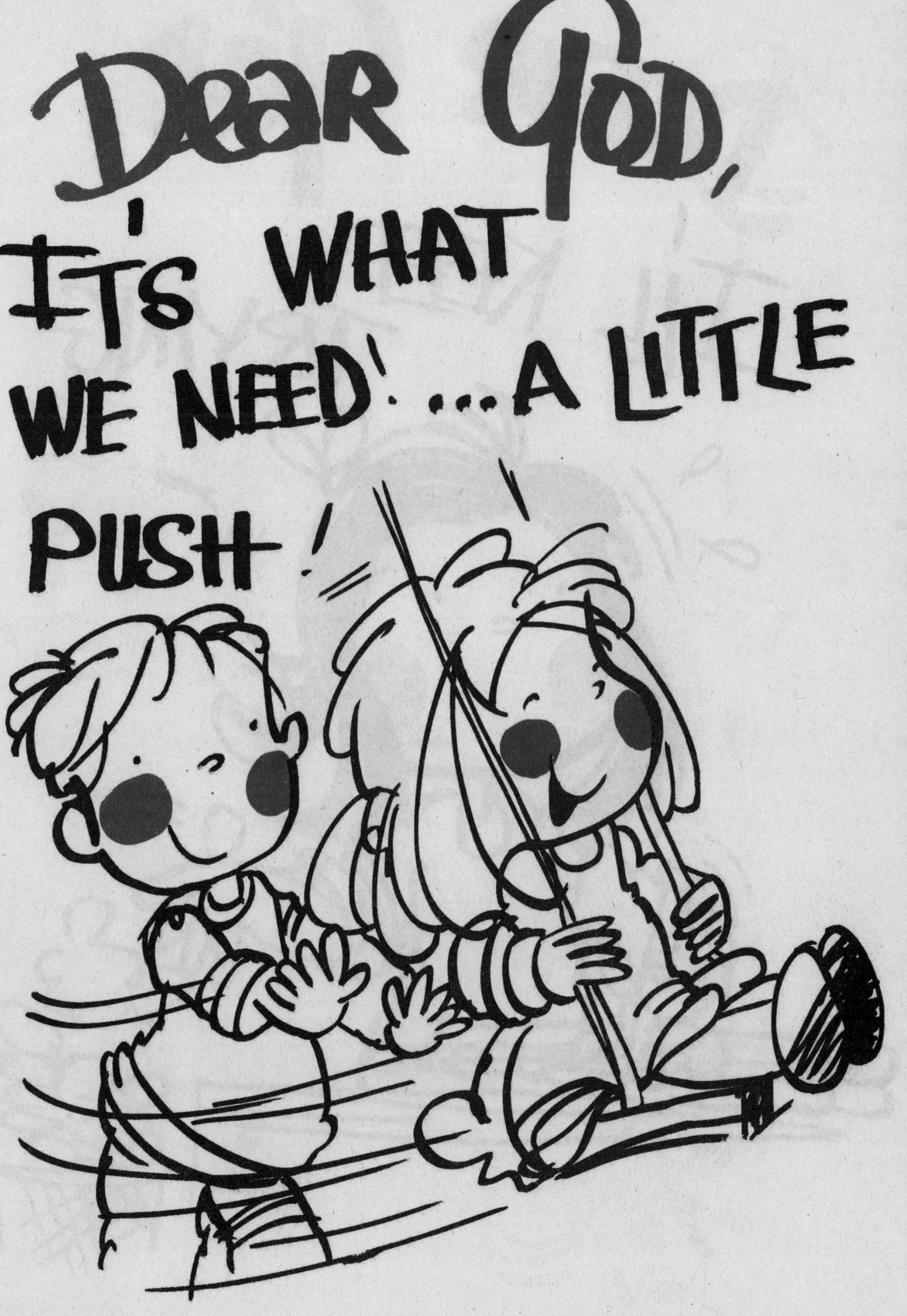
DEAR GOD,
IT'S WHAT WE NEED ...A LITTLE PUSH!

Dear God,
I'll keep trying
Annie

Dear God,
I'll keep trying!

God is happy when you don't give up! He likes it when you continue to do your best to obey His Word. It's not always the easiest thing to keep trying. Sometimes, it's hard to finish your homework or chores. It's hard being nice to people who aren't nice to you. It may seem better just to give in and quit!

But don't do it. Hang in there! Once you've started something, keep at it until you are done. When you're having troubles, trust in God! He will help you to keep trying. Never give up! Keep trusting in God!

Trust in the Lord with all your heart and lean not on your own understanding.

Proverbs 3:5

DEAR GOD,

WE'RE IN THIS TOGETHER!

Dear God,
With Your help we'll make it!

Everyone likes to be on a winning team.
When you are on God's side you'll have all
the help you need! He gives you direction,
safety, and care. He helps you get through
problems, He provides for you, and He loves
you! Thank God for all He does for you!
No matter what you are facing, with God's
help you can make it. God will help you!

*God is our refuge and strength; a very present
help in trouble.*

Psalms 46:1

Dear God,
I THINK I'M IMPROVING!

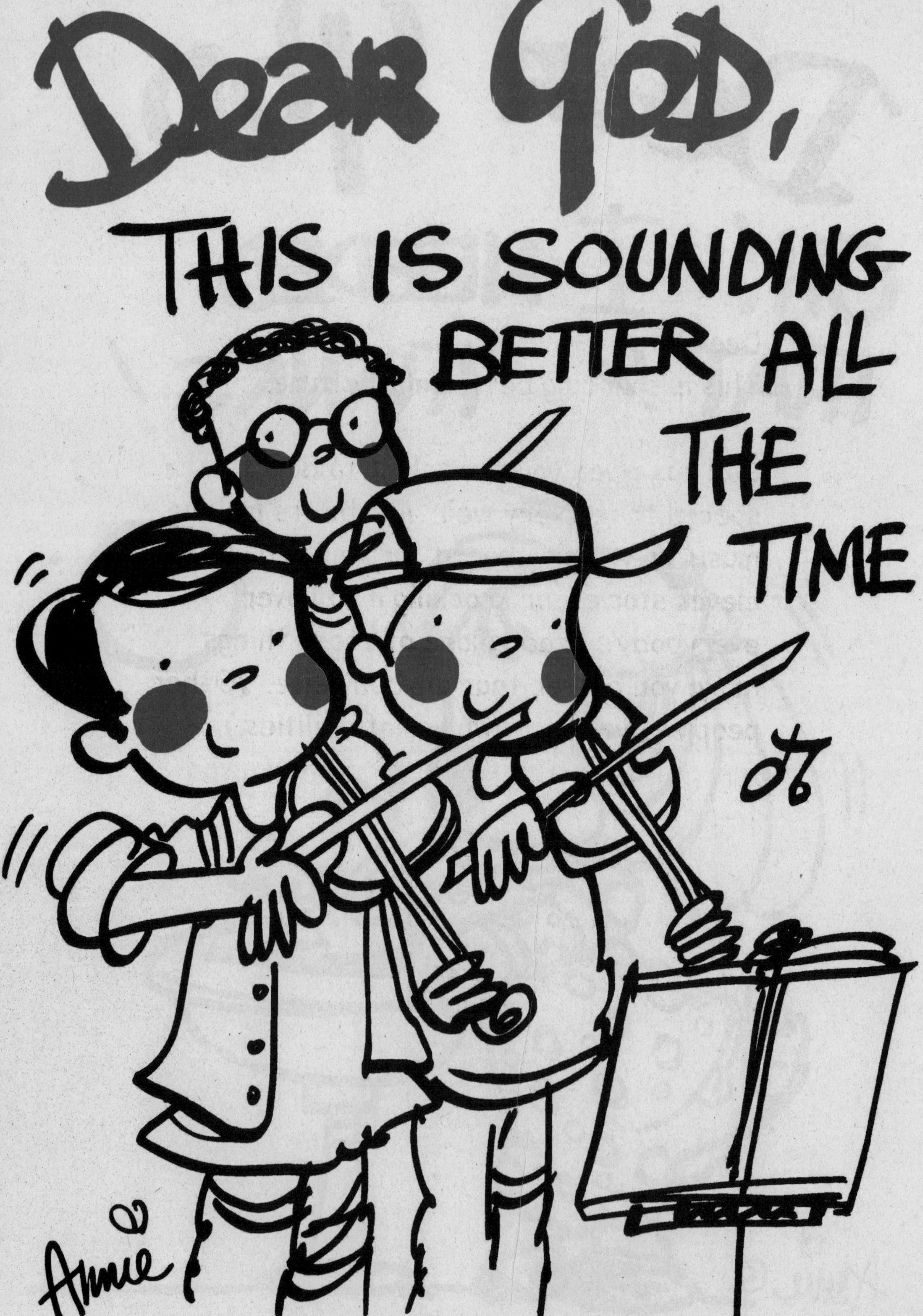
DEAR GOD,
THIS IS SOUNDING BETTER ALL THE TIME
Annie

Dear God,
This is sounding better all the time.

God has given you the talent to do a few
special things very well. Maybe it's making
music on your keyboard, or thinking up
clever stories, or knocking a ball over
everybody's head. None of those things
make you better than anybody else. (Other
people have their own list of abilities.)
But yours are a gift from God. And using
them well is your gift to Him.

Whatsoever thy hand findeth to do,
do it with thy might.
Ecclesiastes 9:10

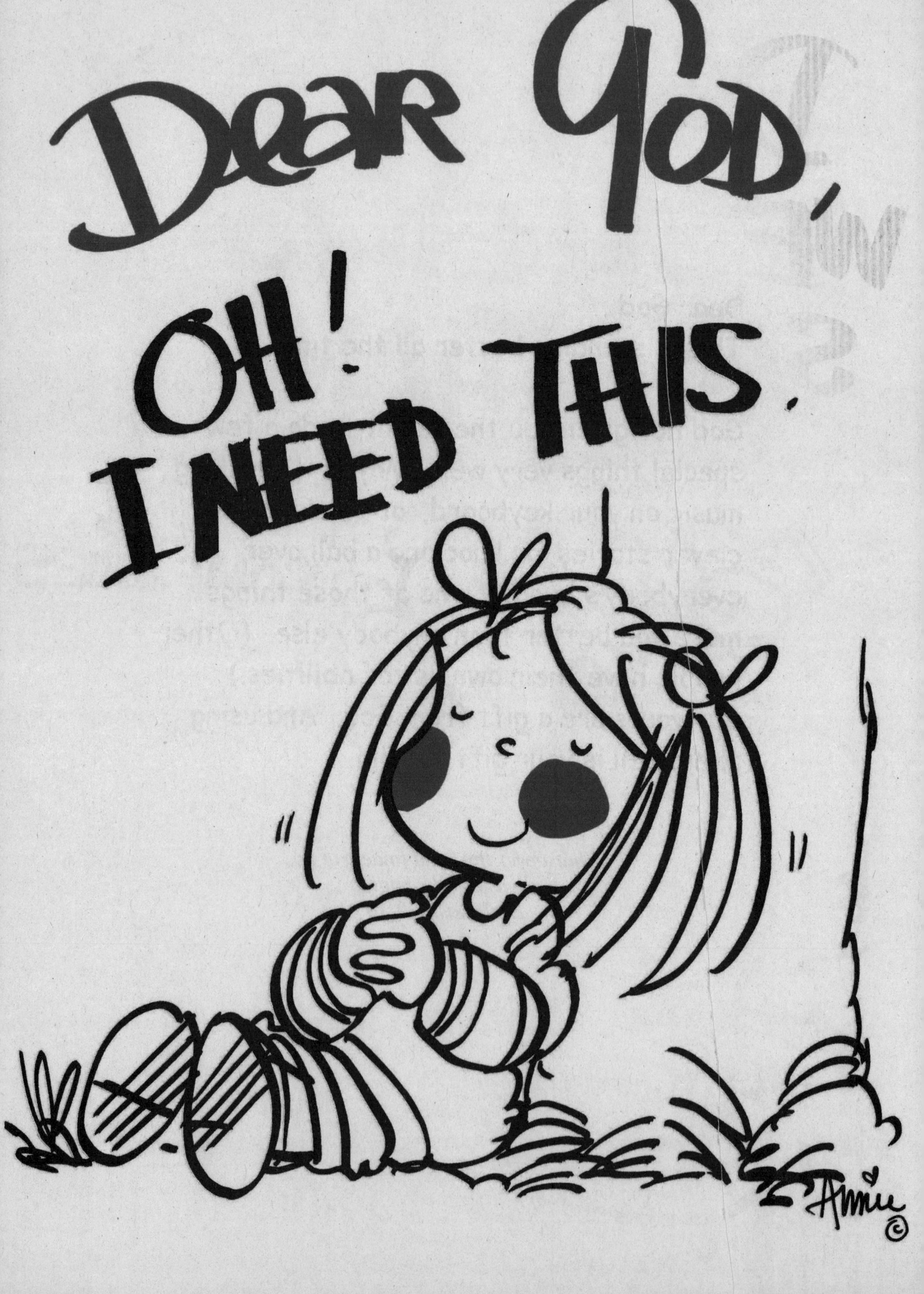
Dear God,
OH! I NEED THIS.
Annie ©

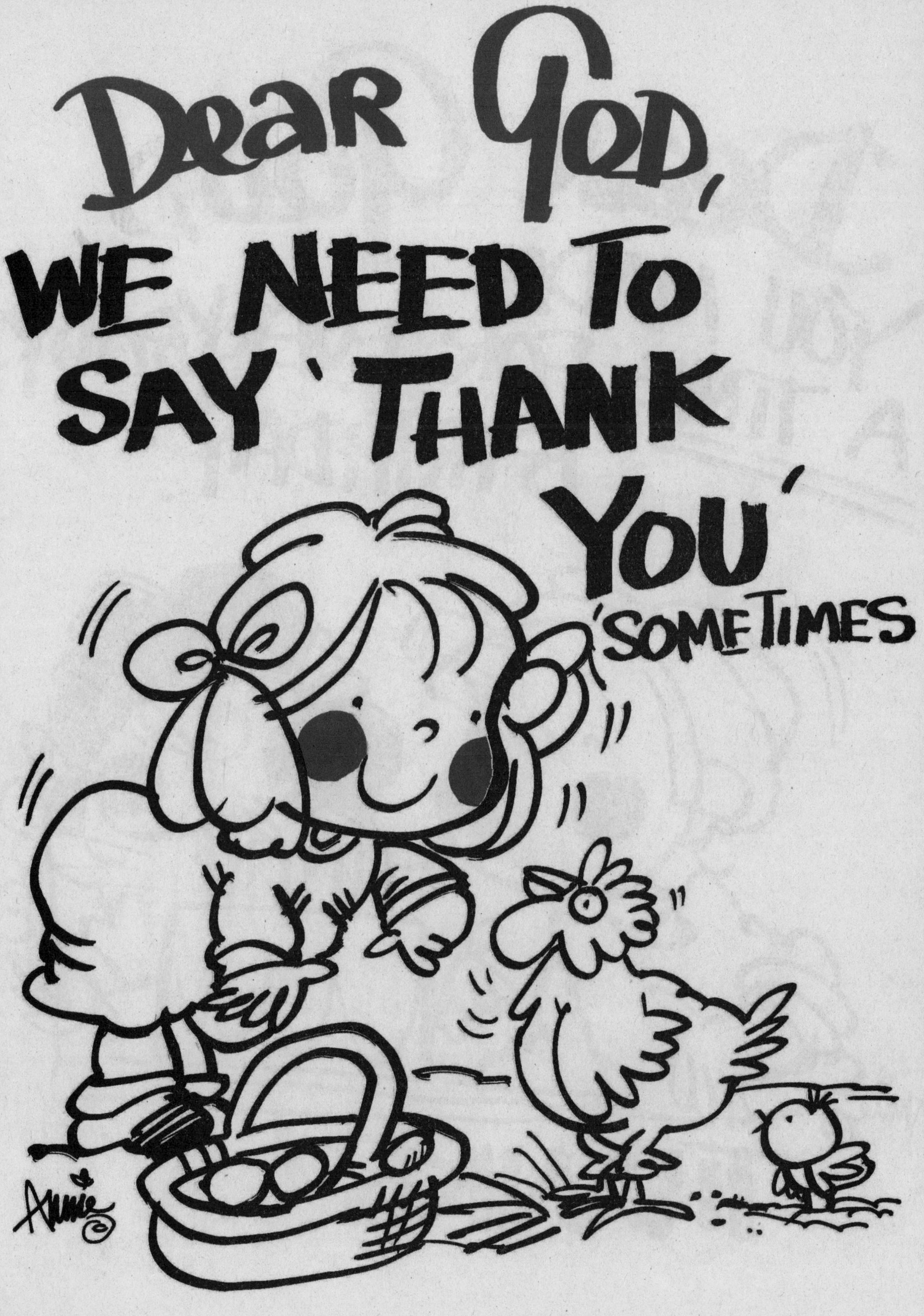
DEAR GOD,
WE NEED TO SAY 'THANK YOU' SOMETIMES
Annie ©

DEAR GOD,

I'M JUST SO HAPPY

Annie

Dear God, THANK YOU FOR BREAKS

Dear God,
Attention everybody! Today is a brand new day and will never be repeated again; it's yours.

Each day is a gift from God. I thank God for this gift. I praise God in the morning. I praise God in the afternoon. I praise God in the evening. I praise God for who He is. I thank God for what He does. The Lord is good. The Lord is worthy of my praise. I remember to thank God for at least five things daily: 1. Life, 2. Food, 3. Home, 4. Family, and 5. Friends.

"This is the day which the Lord hath made; we will rejoice and be glad in it."
Psalm 118:24

DEAR GOD, 'TIS TODAYS, 'TIS ALL I'VE GOT!

NEWS

Dear God,

I'm Making a Splash

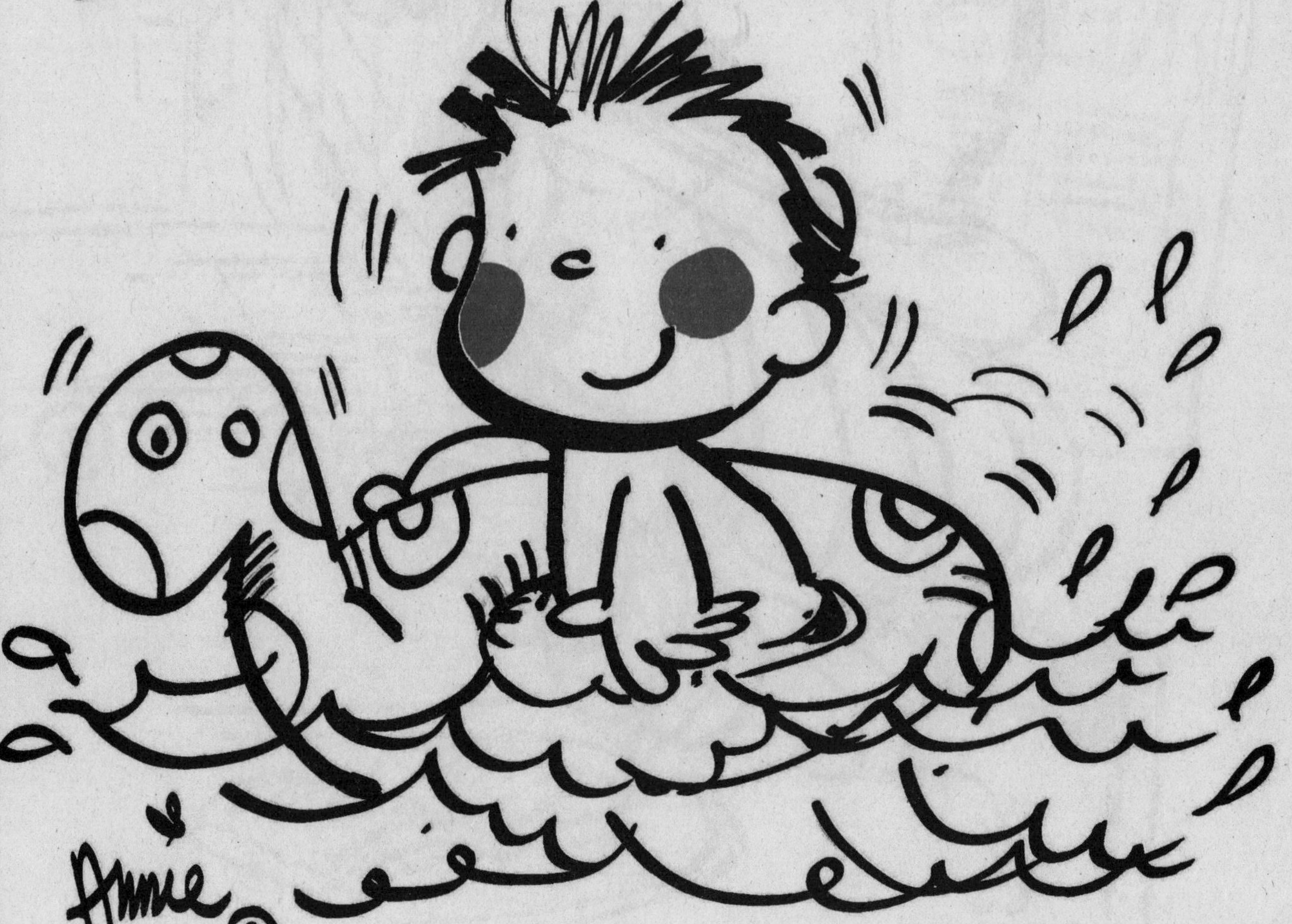

Dear God,

This feels like a good day

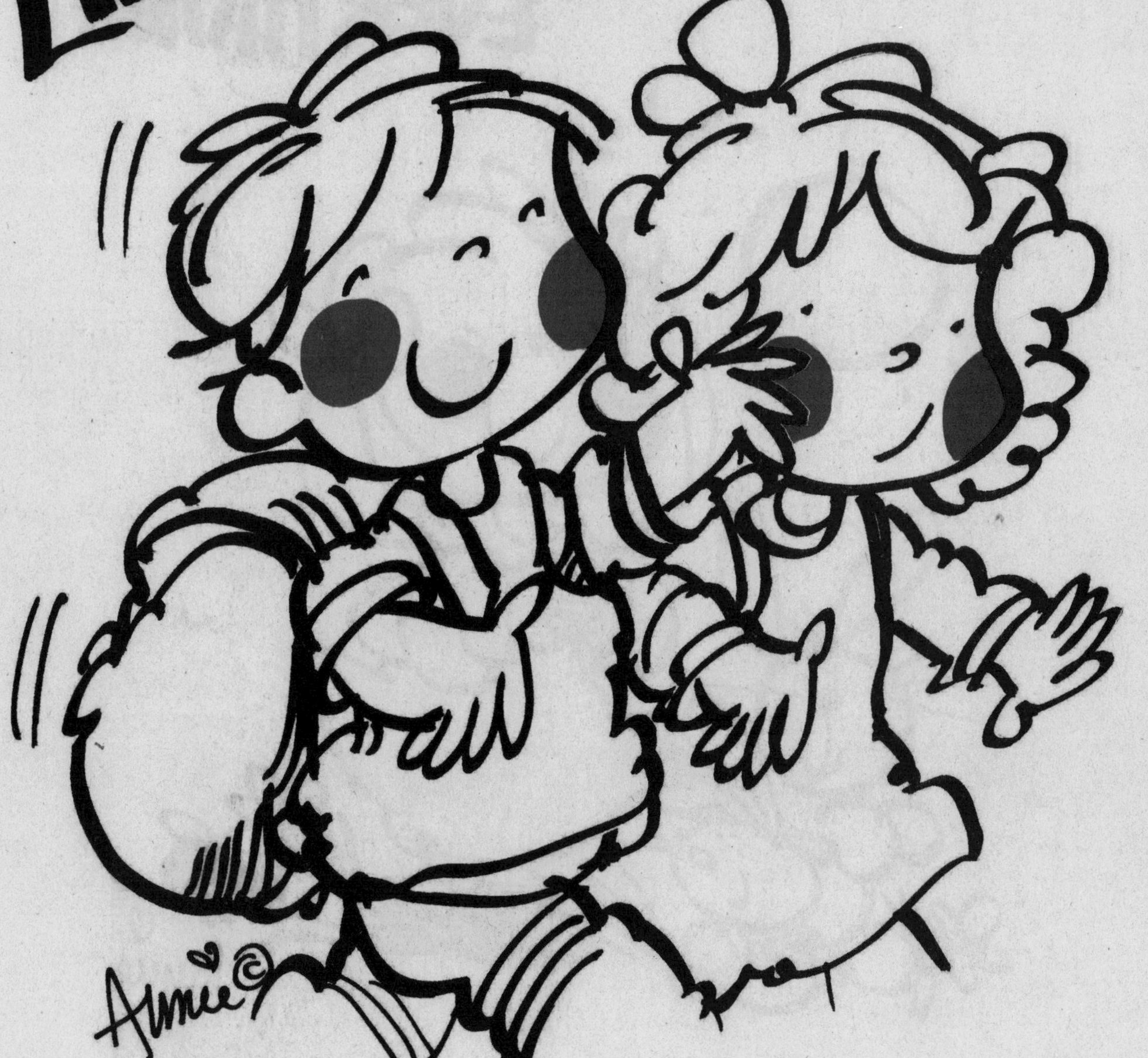

Dear God,

You Thought of Everything

Annie

Dear God,
You thought of everything!

God is so good! He's thought of everything
from petals on flowers to the lashes on your
eyes! He knows everything about you, and
has a wonderful plan for your life. He
thought of the right family and friends
for you. He thought of how you should
breath, eat, sleep, and grow! God loves
thinking about you!

*I know that you can do all things and that no
plan of yours can be ruined.*

Job 42:2 (NCV)

Dear God,

Annie

Dear God,

KEEPING A DIARY IS TERRIFIC... COS YOU MADE EVERY DAY DIFFERENT.

Dear God,
I think I'll dress up today, just in case
you've got something special in mind.

Every morning when you push the covers
back, you're ripping the wrapper off a shiny
new present, a day not quite like any you've
ever lived before or like any you'll live again.
Somehow, God never gets tired of watching
the sun come up, seeing the flowers drip
with dew, or giving you a day like today -
full of all-new things for you to do, to learn,
to enjoy.

But cleave unto the Lord your God,
as ye have done unto this day.
Joshua 23:8

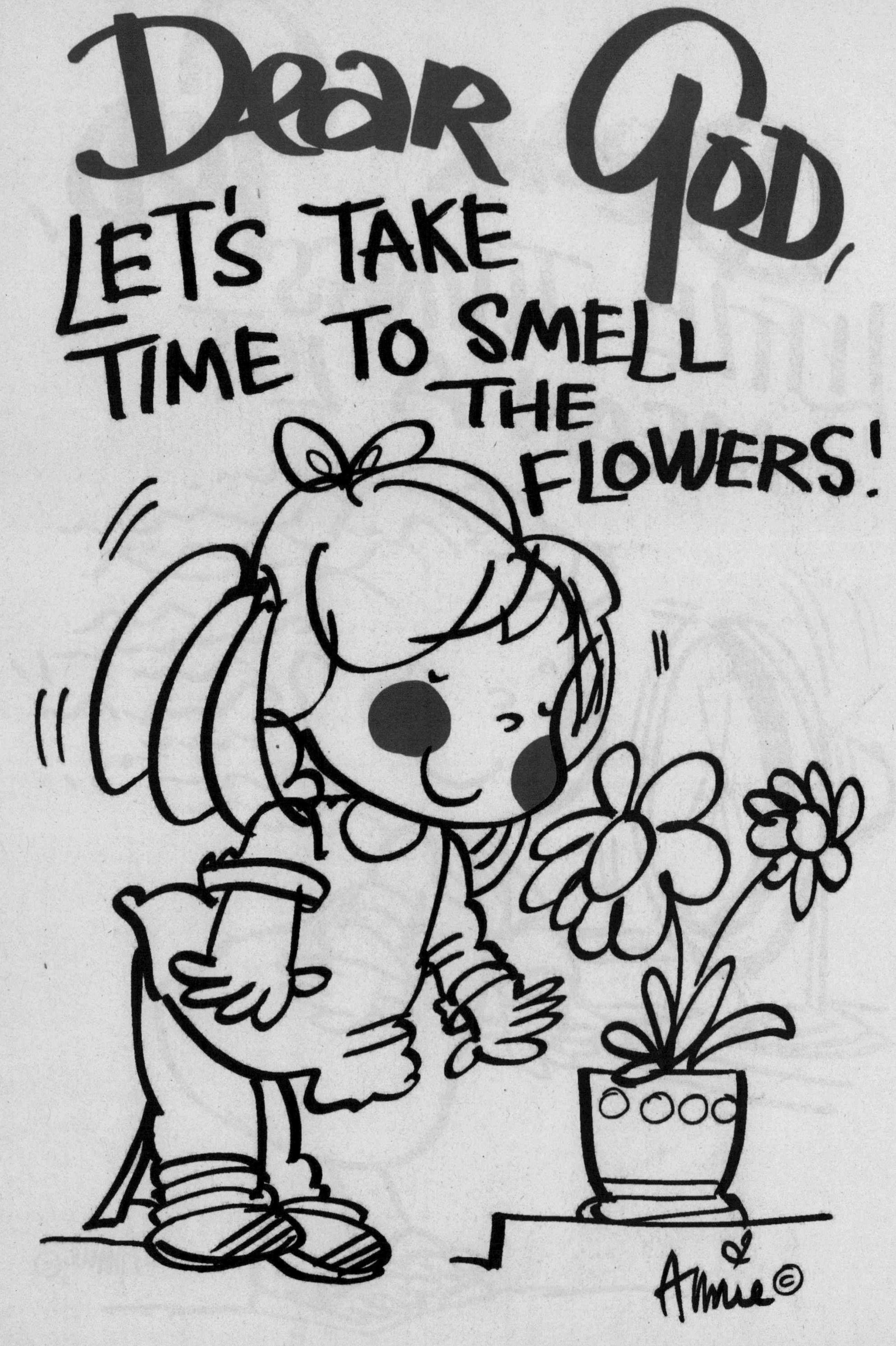
DEAR GOD,
LET'S TAKE TIME TO SMELL THE FLOWERS!
Annie ©

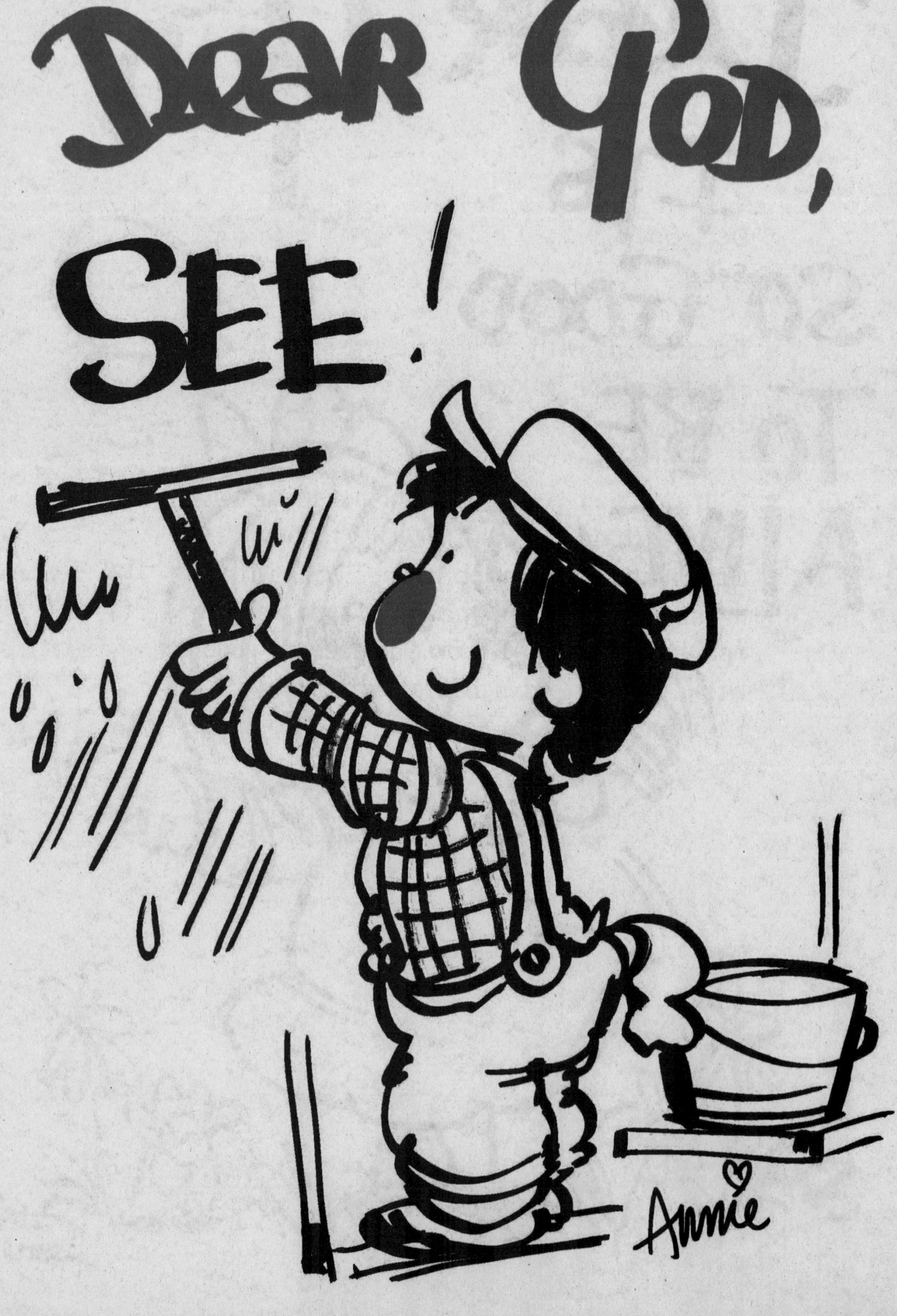
DEAR GOD,
SEE!
Annie

Dear God,
See!

I praise God with my lips and my life. I
thank God for making me. I am different
than anyone else. I thank God for giving me
skill and talent. I have a very special purpose
in life. I thank God for giving me special work
to do each day. I want my work to honor
God. When I have a job to do, I work with all
my might. If I know the job is done well, I
feel happy inside. I know God sees my good
work. I know God is pleased with my life.
I want my life to continually bring praise to
God.

*"And whatsoever ye do in word or deed, do all in the
name of Lord Jesus, giving thanks to
God and the Father by him."*
Colossians 3:17

Dear God,

You know exactly what we need

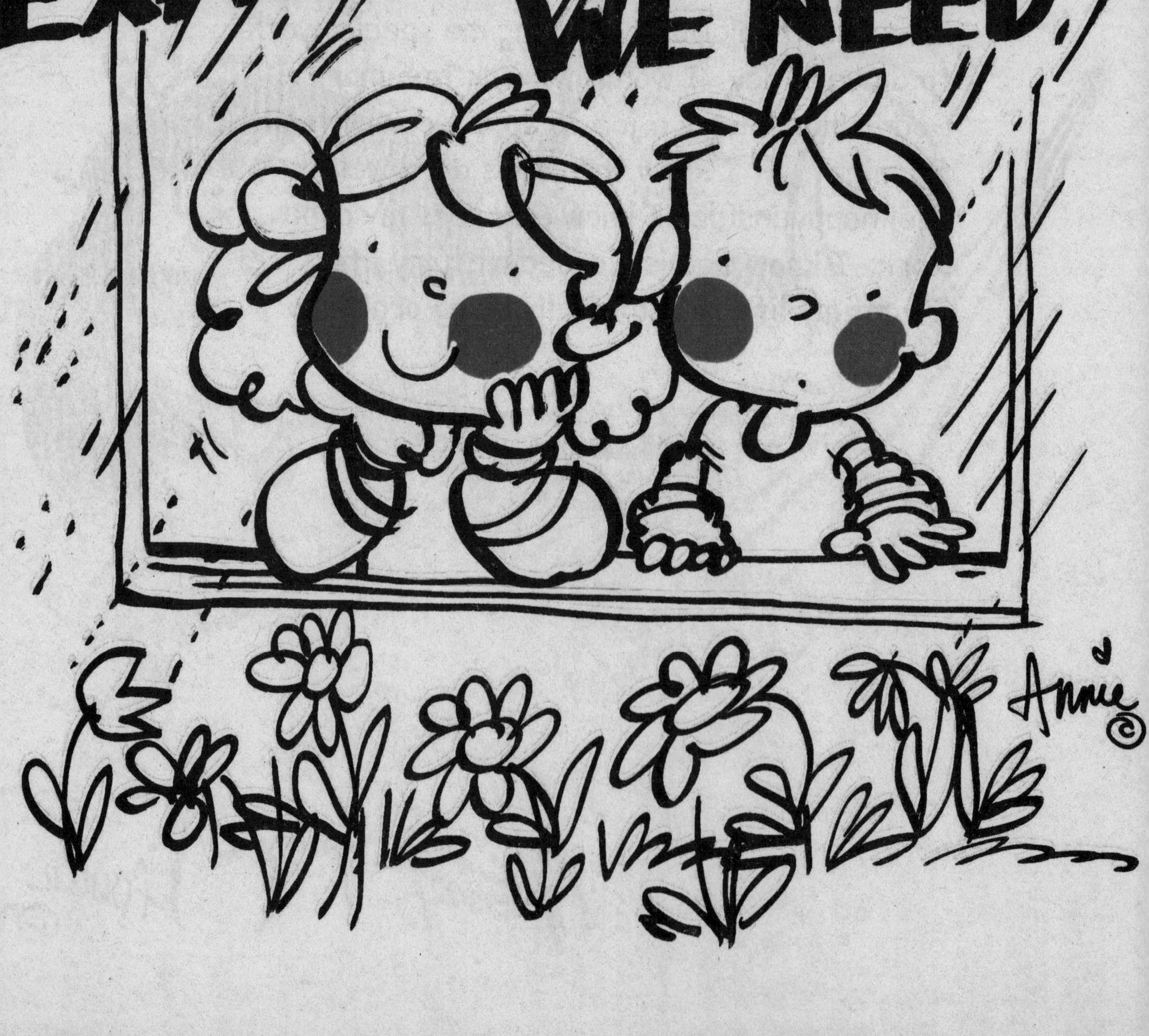

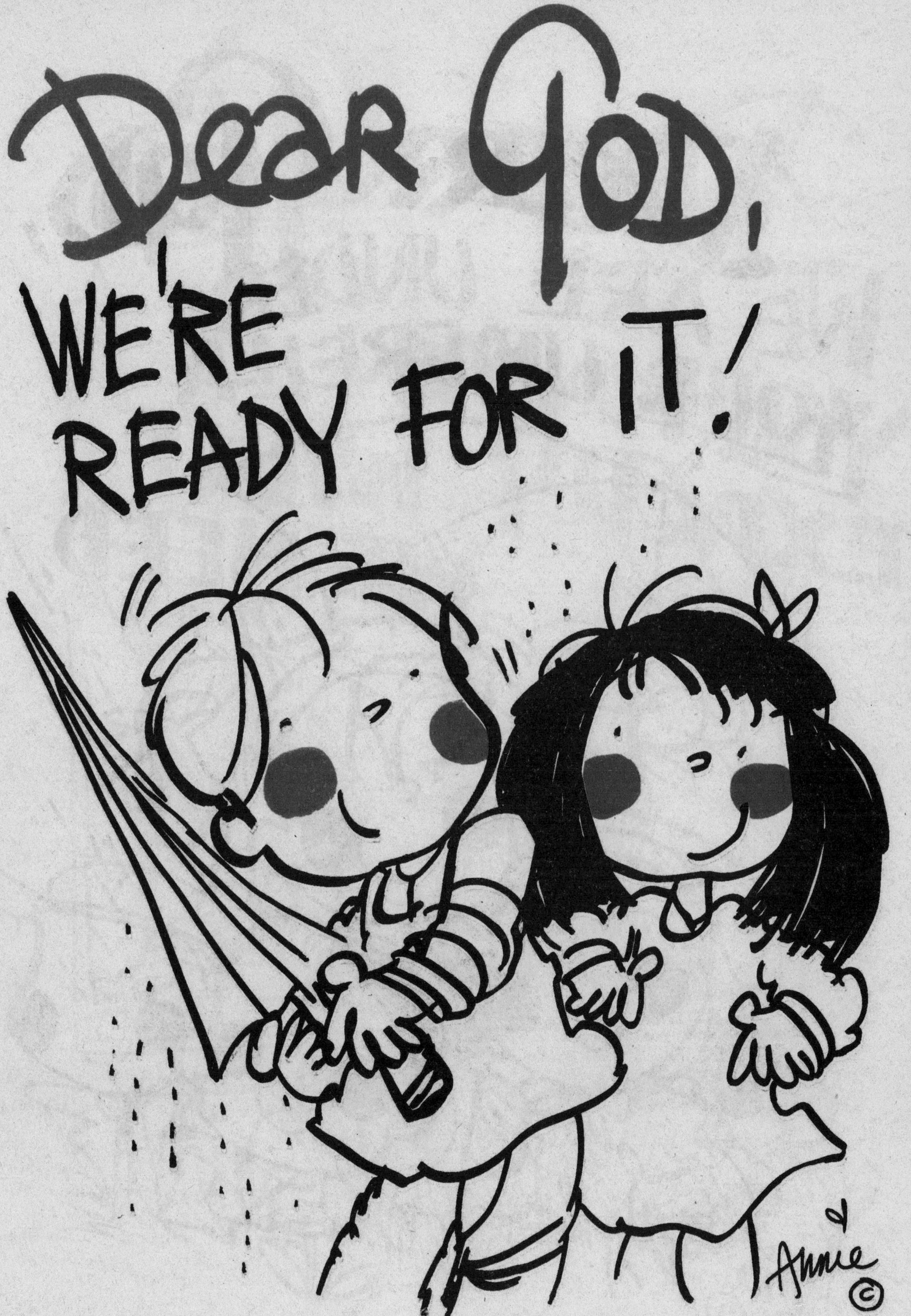
DEAR GOD,
WE'RE READY FOR IT!
Annie ©

DeaR GOD,
JUST A BIT OF
LOVE
AND
CARE

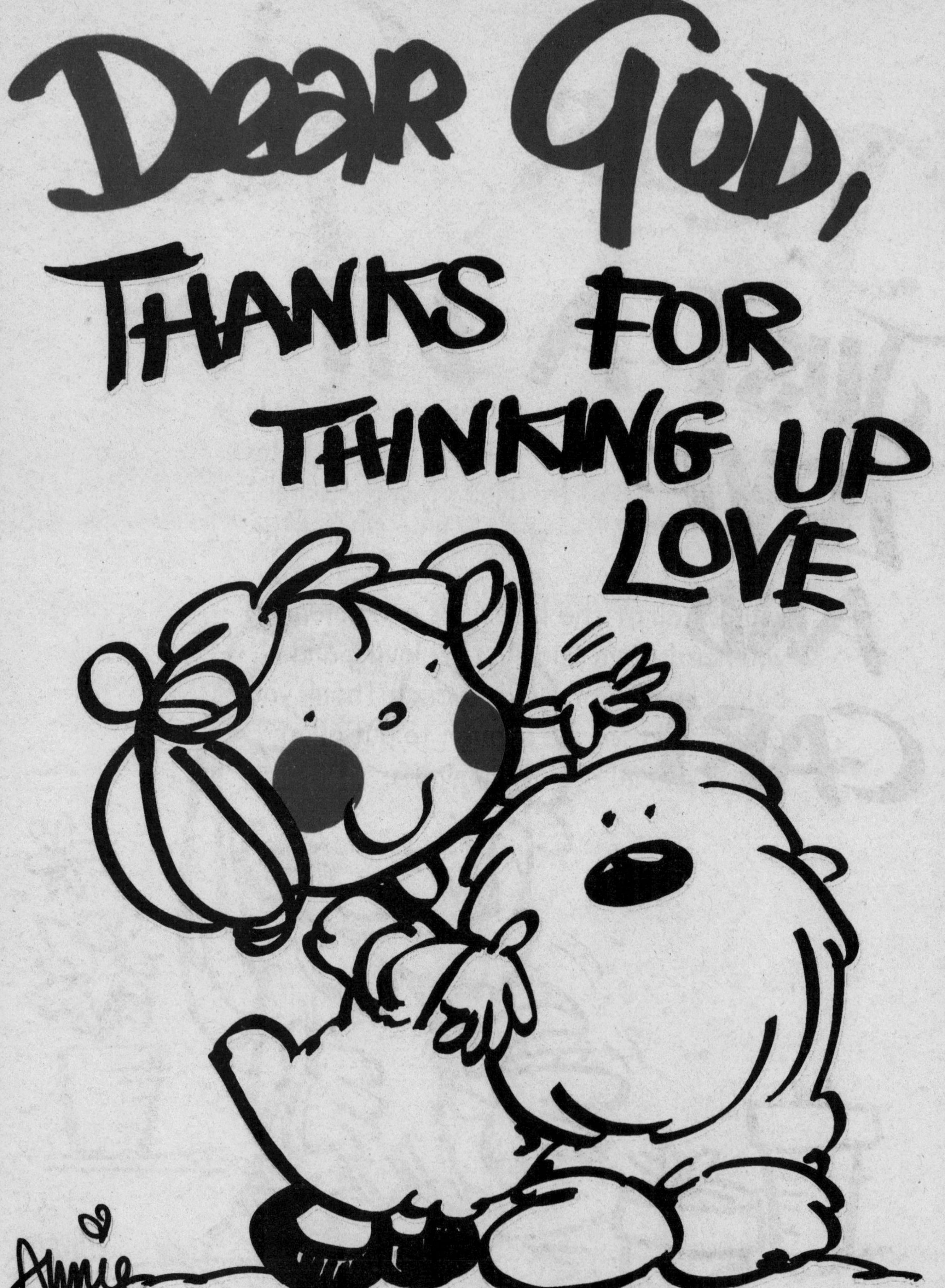
DEAR GOD,
THANKS FOR THINKING UP LOVE
Annie

Dear God,
Thanks for thinking up love.

God has placed wonderful, special people in your life, because He loves you. God's love is perfect. He's thought of everything! Now all you have to do is love Him back, and love others, too. It's that easy! You will get all of the blessings and guidance you need from God just by loving and believing in Him. What a deal! Thank you God, for loving me enough to put all of these special people in my life.

The Lord hath appeared of old unto me, saying,
Yea, I have loved you with an everlasting love.

Jeremiah 31:3

DEAR GOD,

IT'S SO EASY TO LOVE ... WHEN YOU ARE LOVED BACK!

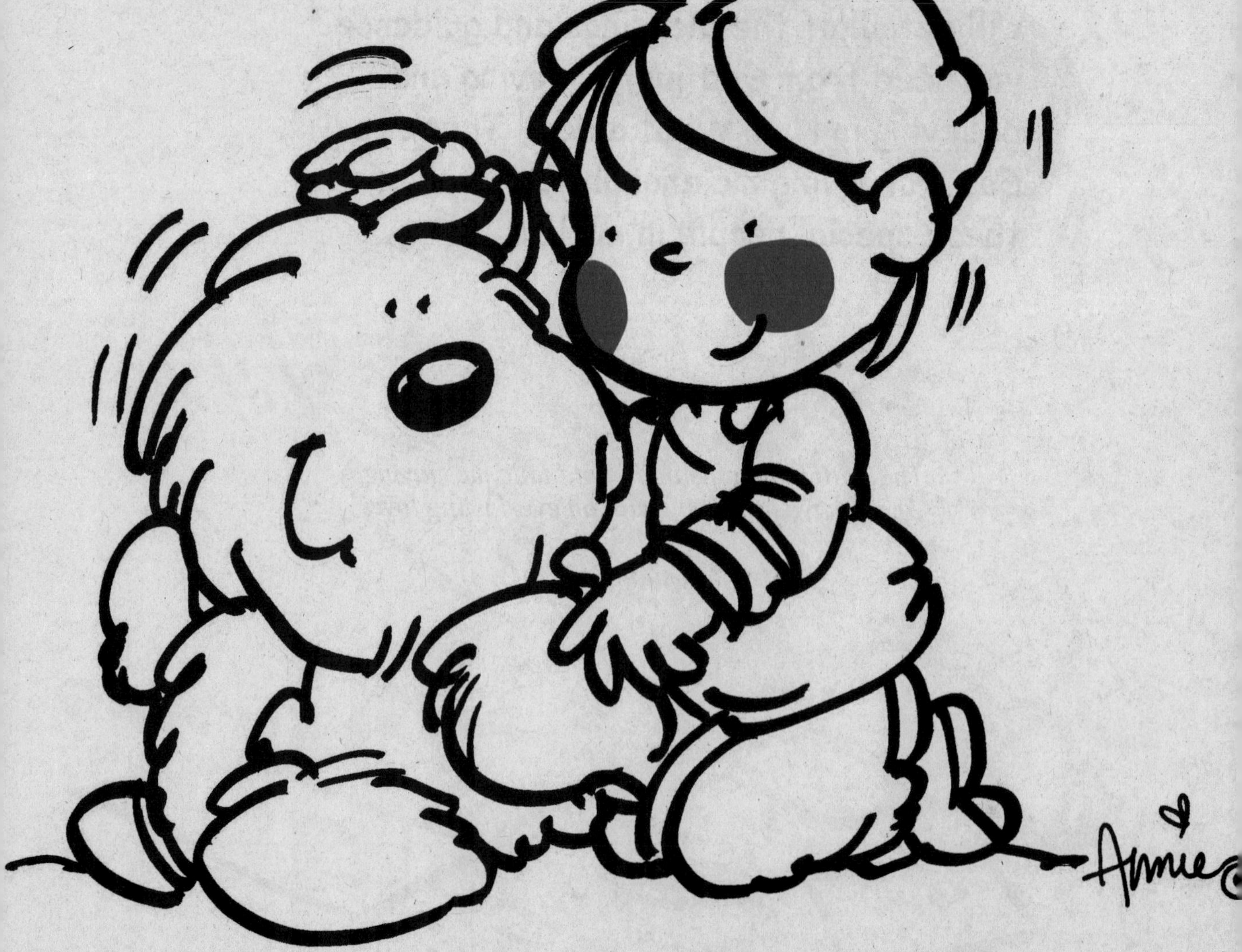

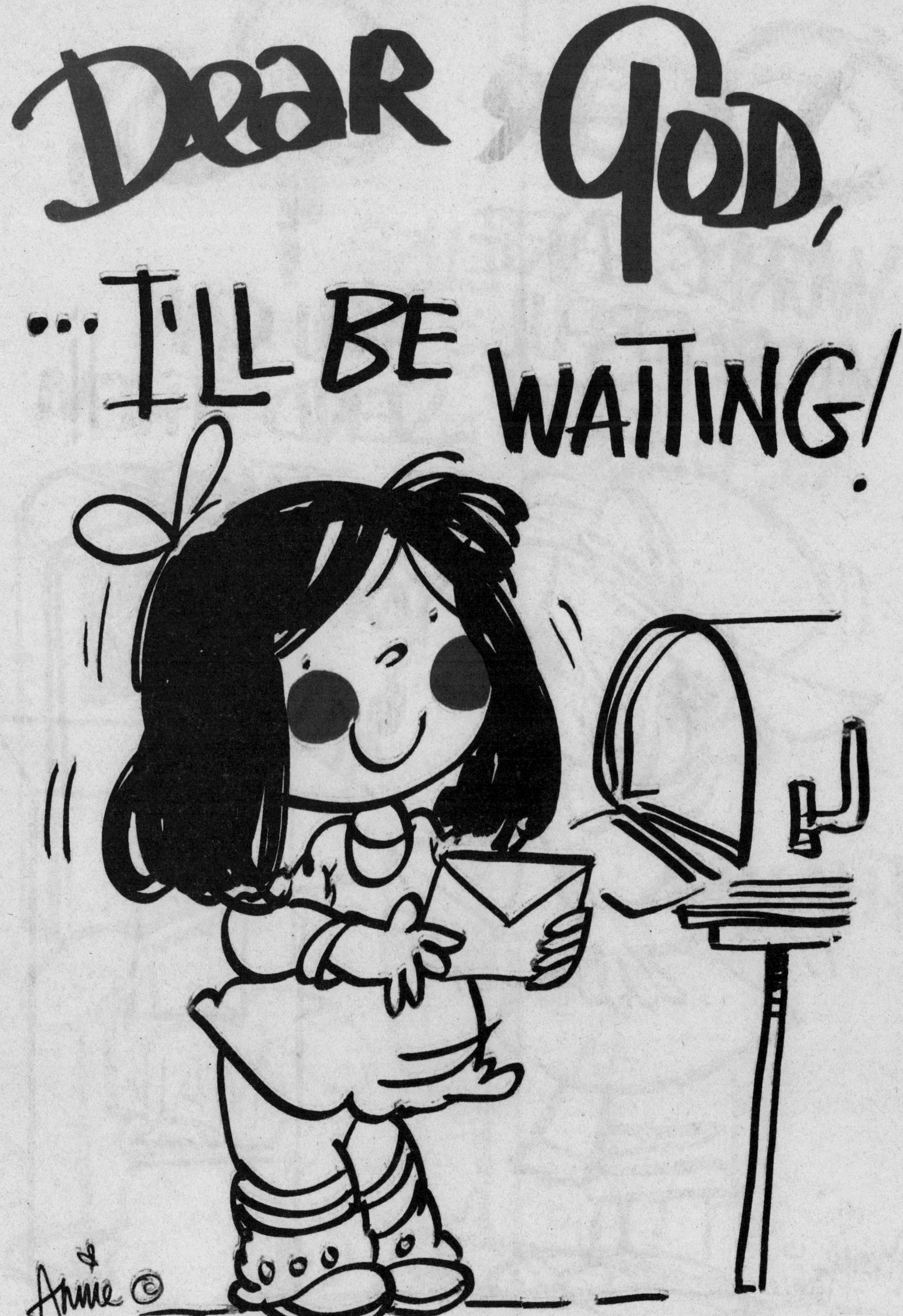
DEAR GOD,
...I'LL BE WAITING!
Annie ©

Dear God,
Words are wonderful...you can always send
them to those you love.

Between that little pink tongue of yours and
those shiny white teeth, you can say any
word you want. Your tongue and your teeth
don't really care what it is. But your friends
do. And God does. Because when you say
kind and helpful words, you give your friends
something to talk about - a friend like you
who really loves them.

*For out of the abundance of the heart
the mouth speaketh.
Matthew 12:34*